W9-CHU-831

DISCARD

Opening Windows

Opening Windows

Confessions of a Canadian Vocal Coach

Stuart Hamilton

DUNDURN
TORONTO

Editor: Allison Hirst
Design: Jesse Hooper
Printer: Trigraphik LBF

Library and Archives Canada Cataloguing in Publication

Hamilton, Stuart
    Opening windows: confessions of a Canadian vocal coach / author, Stuart Hamilton; foreword by Lotfi Mansouri.

Also available in electronic formats.
ISBN 978-1-4597-0512-8

    1. Hamilton, Stuart. 2. Vocal coaches—Canada—Biography. 3. Broadcasters—Canada—Biography. I. Title.

ML429.H222A3 2012   782.1092   C2012-903228-X

1 2 3 4 5   16 15 14 13 12

We acknowledge the support of the **Canada Council for the Arts** and the **Ontario Arts Council** for our publishing program. We also acknowledge the financial support of the **Government of Canada** through the **Canada Book Fund** and **Livres Canada Books**, and the **Government of Ontario** through the **Ontario Book Publishing Tax Credit** and the **Ontario Media Development Corporation**.

Printed and bound in Canada.

VISIT US AT
Dundurn.com | *Definingcanada.ca* | *@dundurnpress* | *Facebook.com/dundurnpress*

Dundurn
3 Church Street, Suite 500
Toronto, Ontario, Canada
M5E 1M2

Gazelle Book Services Limited
White Cross Mills
High Town, Lancaster, England
L41 4XS

Dundurn
2250 Military Road
Tonawanda, NY
U.S.A. 14150

*For all of the singers with whom I've had the privilege of working
over the past seventy years*

Contents

Foreword

Stuart Hamilton is one of the greatest raconteurs I've ever had the pleasure of knowing. Reading this book is like spending a delightful evening in his company as he recounts the tales of his close encounters with the denizens of the opera world. It is told with all his wit, charm, and intelligence, as well as his great knowledge and love of music and artists.

From his early days as a young rebel in Regina, through his struggles to get started in Toronto, and finally his recognition as one of Canada's musical leaders, this is a thoroughly enjoyable account of the development of opera in Canada and his own enormous contributions to that development. It will indeed "open windows" for his readers.

Lotfi Mansouri
Former general director of the Canadian Opera Company
and the San Francisco Opera

July 2011
San Francisco

Photo by Janet Stubbs.

Lotfi Mansouri (right) and the author, April 2009.

Acknowledgements

Several people were a great help during the writing of this book. I'd like to thank John Stanley and Helmut Reichenbaecher for nagging me to put pen to paper in the first place. I am grateful to Margaret McKelvey and the late Mary Alice Rogers for their invaluable editorial advice. Thanks also to Wayne Gooding, who took time away from his all-consuming job as editor of *Opera Canada* magazine to make sense of my rather chaotic first chapter. And most of all I have to thank the beautiful Maria Kastellitz, whose enthusiasm and faith in the book never wavered.

The book wouldn't have happened without all of you.

Preface

One day at a piano lesson, I said to my teacher, Alberto Guerrero, "You must be very proud to have been the teacher of Glenn Gould."

"No," he replied. "Glenn would have been great no matter with whom he had studied. If I'm proud of anything in my life, it is that I was able to open a few windows onto the world of music for the less talented students who worked with me."

Guerrero was a magnificent musician and a constant inspiration. Many things he told me have illuminated my life, but the remark about the window opening has stuck with me through over sixty years of coaching singers. This book is an effort to recount my experiences as I tried to live up to Guerrero's "Opening Windows."

Chapter 1

A Shaky Start

"Down by the sea shore, shimmer, shimmer,
There stood a maiden, slimmer, slimmer.
False buck teeth and her hair p'roxided,
There in the moonlight, she looked lopsided.
Ruffles on her petticoat, ruf'lin in the breezes
Sounds like sandpaper rus'lin on her kneeses.
Things like this that women do—
S'nough to make a man leave home—
Without a shirt!"

— "The Glow Worm"

Okay, so it's not Schubert, but it's what I grew up with. If you're wondering how someone raised on songs like that went on to have a thrilling career as a vocal coach to opera singers who sang in all the great opera houses of the world, and who was accompanist for some of the world's greatest recitalists of the second half of the twentieth century, read on.

Once I decided to be a musician I never had any doubts about it, but looking back I'm not at all sure that I realized it would take over my life in the way that it did.

I was not born into a musical family. My father's efforts to carry a tune were not appreciated by the rest of the congregation at the First Presbyterian Church in Regina — a church that he frequented rarely, by the way.

We had a piano, as almost everyone did in the 1930s, but no one ever played it. Well, hardly ever. Occasionally my mother would "render" a version of "There's a Long, Long Trail A-Winding," a song from the First World War. The problem was, she never changed the harmony in the base. And then there was my older sister, Dorothy, who was forced to take piano lessons for a while. She got as far as "The Glow Worm" (for the unauthorized lyrics, see above), but then, to everyone's immense relief, she threw it over. At the age of five, I deduced the relationship between the hammers of the piano and the hammer in the tool box and, putting two and two together as it were, took the tool box one and slammed the keys of the piano to make the ones in the instrument jump and bang. As the keys were made of ivory, my efforts resulted in many a torn finger later in life.

I was born in the city of Regina, then, as now, the capital of the province of Saskatchewan on the Canadian Prairies. The year was 1929 and I arrived on the 28th of September, about ten days before the great economic crash. In later years, my father, not with malice but with frustration at having to deal with someone he couldn't understand, had two expressions: "You give me pain where I should have pleasure." — It took me a long time to figure that one out — and "You brought on the crash."

My parents had moved to Regina the year before I was born. Father, James Shier Hamilton, thirty-one years old in 1928, was a lawyer in a village south of Regina called Ceylon (population in 2009: 105). He had received an offer to work for the Sterling Trust Corporation, which had its home base in Toronto and a regional office in Regina. It was a great step up for Dad and he was assured that there were unlimited opportunities for advancement, so he moved his family — wife Florence Stuart, aged thirty-four, and their three children, eight-year-old Peter, six-year-old Dorothy, and five-year-old Douglas — to the big city (population in 1928: 45,000). He put a down payment on a small house about a fifteen-minute walk from his downtown office, and at Christmas he got his wife pregnant again.

Then I appeared and the stock market crashed. The staff at the Sterling Trust was reduced to Dad, his boss, and a secretary. Dad's salary was cut back to $125 per month, plus the use of a company car.

Obviously, we were very poor, but I was never aware of it. My parents never gave their children the impression that things were desperate, although it must have been a tremendous struggle to keep going. Mother told me later that they were grateful that Dad had a job at all, as so many people were out of work, or "on relief," as the government dole was called.

I was never close to my parents. They were good people, even noble in the way they handled the terrible economic strains of raising five children during the Great Depression. It was just that there was next to no intellectual stimulation at home. There were no books: Mother read *Ladies Home Journal*. Dad never seemed to read anything. He was passionately interested in politics. I remember him hovering over the radio listening to Hitler's speeches and predicting unmentionable horrors, which the "madman" was about to unleash onto the world, predictions that, alas, were all too accurate. None of this interested me. Through the movies I sensed that there was something else to life and that something else was what I was aiming for.

The day I was born, my father was in the hospital, where doctors were trying to remove a little bone from a pork chop that had lodged in his throat. The family had all

I was born about ten days before the great economic crash of 1929. Here I am in 1930, svelte as always.

It was 1934, about the time that my sister Dorothy took me to the movies for the first time — my life was transformed.

wished for a girl to balance the two boys and one girl already there, so apparently there were general lamentations when I turned out to be male. The physician who delivered me, a Dr. Whetham, told my mother that I was so beautiful that he would take me if they didn't want another boy. (I have always considered myself to be a Great Beauty, but when I look at photos of myself, I think there must be something wrong with the camera.)

One way or another they decided to keep me. Dorothy has said that I was a cheerful and contented baby. I certainly look well-fed in photographs of the period.

I had varying degrees of success with my siblings. I hardly got to know Peter. By the time I was ten he had left to join the air force for Second World War service, and when he returned home he got married and started a family. Everyone loved Peter. He wasn't exactly handsome, but he was tall, with beautiful black curly hair that he got from our mother. (The rest of us were straight-haired blonds like Dad.) The most important thing about him was his charm. He was one of those people who could walk into a room and be friends with everyone, no matter how heterogeneous the company. Much later, I was to benefit enormously from his good nature and generosity.

I adored my sister Dorothy. She turned out to have a superb contralto voice and it was because of her that I later became a musician.

My poor brother Doug I detested, as he did me. I say "poor" because he had to live in the shadow of Peter's radiance and under the shadow of my enmity. I later realized how unjust my loathing for him was, but by that time it was too late.

When my younger sister Patricia came along in 1937 she was simply something that had to be dealt with. Now, of course, she is one of Canada's most accomplished and distinguished actresses, but at that time, who knew? She just got in my way at first.

For the first ten years of my life, Regina was a cultural desert, and because of the Great Drought it was a physical one as well. Seventy years later, one can see that the Prairies are prosperous and beautiful in a certain way, but in those days they were desolate.

The dust storms! I remember that, before going to school in the morning, our job was to dust everything in the house; and then, coming home for lunch, we had to do it all over again because by that time there was another inch of dust on *everything*. And the grasshoppers! We couldn't wear shorts in the heat of the summer because if you walked or ran through a vacant lot, your legs were covered with the horrid little buggers.

For me, the worst thing was the sense of isolation. One had the feeling that elsewhere in the world something interesting was happening but that you were never going to be a part of it.

We did have a cottage about a hundred miles from Regina where we would spend the summer months. It took a whole day to get there by car if one didn't slide into the ditch on the side of the road. Unfortunately, this happened fairly often, given the primitive conditions of the roads in those days. When it did, it involved a lot of alarming pushing and grunting to get the car back on the road. This pushing and grunting frightened us all, and we worried about the survival of my poor father.

When we finally arrived, we would rejoice in the trees (on the Prairies it was what passed for a wooded area — forget about a forest) and, oh, miracle in those times of total lack of water, a lake! One in which one could actually swim, as opposed to the puddle in Regina, which had been dug out of nothing to reflect the very handsome legislative building, and

Christmas, 1945. (Left to right) Doug, Dad, Dorothy, Patricia, Peter, Mom, and me. Peter and Doug had just returned from the war. Mom and Patricia both had the flu.

which, if one were intrepid, one could walk across without ever getting one's knees wet.

Actually, our lake was very pretty, with crystal clear water and many fish. I revisited the lake in 1995 and was horrified to see that due to mismanagement it had shrunk to less than half its former size and was totally devoid of fish.

At first, I loved going to the lake, and I loved the change from the baking city. However, it turns out that I'm a city person after all, and eventually I resented having to spend two months in "Green Hell." I wanted to be where the action was, although "action" used in connection with Regina in the thirties and forties is something of an oxymoron.

From a cultural standpoint, the movies were everything — the *only* thing. When I was five years old, Dorothy took me to the Capitol Theatre to see a matinee of a Shirley Temple movie in which she sang "On the Good Ship Lollipop," and bang, my life was transformed. I wanted to be up there on the screen with Shirley and Jeanette MacDonald and Nelson Eddy singing their songs and being off the Prairies and being part of the Big World that I thought was out there waiting for me.

I soon learned to do imitations of Mae West and Greta Garbo that were thought to be hilariously cute by adults, but which were received with decidedly less enthusiasm by my playmates. For the first five or six years of school, I would invite one after the other of the boys in my class to play at my house, where they would be my servants or slaves and I would be the queen. I went through a lot of boys that way.

If the movies were GOOD, then everything else — Sunday school, Cubs (the junior version of the Boy Scouts), and school — was BAD. These latter activities involved being part of a group, and that's not what I had in mind for my life.

My search for self-fulfillment began with singing. Graduating from "Down by the sea shore, shimmer, shimmer," I joined a boys' choir and, because my voice was very pretty, I was soon promoted to soloist. I was very undisciplined as a singer. I wasn't interested in the technique, I just wanted to get up and emote (something that would dog me throughout my musical career).

Each year, the Saskatchewan Music Teachers' Association mounted a music festival. It was a highlight of the musical life of Regina. Several adjudicators would be brought from England (Canada in those days was still, in many people's minds, a colony of the British Empire) and there were three or four days of intense competition, especially in the piano and voice categories.

My particular brand of emoting didn't go down with the adjudicators, and I always came in second or third. Finally, in my third year of competing in the boy soprano class, the last year before my voice broke, Mother said to me, "You have to sing the song like you mean it and don't be so self-conscious about how you look." The song that year was "Johnny Wagger," a song about a sheepdog. Now, I'm not and never have been an animal person. The only place I like to see them is on the television where they eat one another. However, I was determined to prove that I could adore that dog better than anyone else, so I got up and sang the song as if it were *Elektra*. Of course, I won.

Another of my triumphs in those days was "Je suis Titania" from *Mignon* by Ambroise Thomas. Of course, one of the most demanding arias for coloratura soprano was not on the syllabus of the festival. No, I sang it at Kinsmen and Lions Club luncheons before a lot of bemused business-men. I had learned the piece from a record of Lily Pons (we didn't have a record player, but I had a friend who did). I didn't know a word of French in those days, but I figured that Lily, being French, should know what she was doing, so I copied her sound-for-sound.

After one particularly dazzling rendition, a man came up to me and asked me if I knew what I was saying in the aria. I, of course, admitted that I didn't. He said, "The first line you say is 'Yes, for this evening, I am queen of the fairies.'"

I waited for him to go on.

"Well, do you think that's an appropriate thing for a boy to be singing?" he asked.

I said, "Why not?" After all, I was eleven or twelve, and this was 1942 in Regina. Now, of course, I understand what he was trying to say, but at that time I didn't know anything about those things, so I continued my performances, forgetting about this crank.

Unsure of my destiny, and thrashing around for some cultural outlet, I wasn't closing any doors, and I felt that I might have a brilliant future in figure skating. Of course, with this discipline, technique is all-important.

As usual, that didn't stop me. I could twirl like a madman. I billed myself (or more precisely, I was billed) as "The Human Top."

While I certainly could twirl, it turns out that something else was wanted as well. I had an adorable little Billy Bee costume, yellow with brown spots, plus two little antennae. The people at the club where I skated finally convinced me that in spite of the terrible cuteness of my routine, they didn't feel that I really had a future as a skater, due, I suspect, to crass jealousy on their part. However, never one to hang around where I wasn't appreciated, I did my farewell performance at the age of eleven and moved on (as it were.)

The Theatre beckoned. I was a child actor along with my other accomplishments. However, I was not happy with the roles in which they saw fit to cast me. I was thought to be funny and was always cast as the character comic creature. I had success with this, but my soul longed to be cast as "the boy." When I spoke to the woman who ran the theatre about this, she rasped, "Listen kid. The way you act, you're lucky you don't get cast as 'the girl.'"

After this calculated bit of effrontery, I decided that The Theatre was not where I belonged, and I withdrew, leaving them bereft of their comic star.

Up until then, music had been very peripheral to my activities. Singing had been fun, but my voice, when it broke, precluded a career in that line. By the time I was twelve, Dorothy was developing into a major talent, and so I began bugging my parents for piano lessons so that I could accompany her when she sang. Right from the start, for me, the piano was a vehicle for associating with singers. I never entertained any ambitions as a solo pianist. However, at the same time, I also desperately wanted a bicycle. As I mentioned, we were anything but rich, so my parents said that it was one thing or the other, so I chose the piano lessons, knowing that the next year I would in all probability get the bike. Which is exactly what happened.

The Conservatory of Music in Regina was a small building, in the basement of which were a group of rabbit warrens where about eight or ten women taught piano and voice. It was in no way a music school in the sense of Julliard in New York or the Paris Conservatoire. When I tried to enroll with the teacher who had been recommended to me, I was told that she was fully booked, but that a pupil of hers would be available. I don't know what this pupil had been up to, but it certainly wasn't music. When, at my first lesson, I played "The Puppet's Prayer," or something equally sappy, at the end of the piece there was the sign that means "pause." It's one of the most common signs in music, but I knew nothing, and I said to this girl, "What does that mean?" She said, "Um, I don't know. I'll have to go home and look it up." And I (or rather, my father) was paying twenty-five cents for *this*? Outrageous! When my parents complained, the conservatory suddenly discovered that the original teacher had just had a cancellation and could take me as a pupil after all.

What a difference! This new teacher had ideas, technical and musical, and she seemed to have all the answers. I immediately fell in love with her, but after three lessons she announced that she was expecting a "blessed event" and was passing me on to another "excellent" teacher.

She wasn't kidding about the excellent part. The new teacher turned out to be a stunningly beautiful Norwegian woman named Helen Dahlstrom. Again, I fell madly in love. She was tough, very disciplined, and she knew her stuff. I was thrilled with her lessons and I progressed rapidly. But then she announced that she and her husband were moving to British Columbia and that she was passing me on to the best teacher in Regina and that I would be very happy with her.

Martha Somerville Allan was a formidably beautiful woman and a magnificent pianist. I had heard her play the first movement of the Grieg Piano Concerto with the little conservatory orchestra and had been bowled over by the power and musical sweep of her performance. Unfortunately, she had a strange problem with her skin, which dried out around her nails and opened horribly painful cracks that made it almost impossible for her to play. The Grieg was the last time she played in public, but she would occasionally play for me at our lessons. She had studied in Chicago with the legendary Rudolf Ganz and she had a remarkable command of the repertoire.

Alas! By the time I got to work with her, she was trying to have a baby and she cancelled many lessons. Finally, she became pregnant and retired from teaching until after the safe arrival of the baby. I was once again passed on to a very talented pupil of hers named Dorothy Schmidt. Dorothy was more of a pal than a teacher. I loved our lessons, tons of laughs, but they really were more fun than disciplined work.

Meanwhile, there was always the dreaded school. Looking back, I really don't quite know why I hated it so much. I have never liked being told what to do, but I think it was more than that. I didn't like any of my schoolmates. I was the classic loner. I wanted to be playing the piano and that's all.

A team from an American university came through Western Canada doing a massive survey with IQ tests. I wasn't happy doing it — "If one train leaves the station going such and such miles an hour and another leaves, etc. etc.": *Who cares?*

Of course, that's not the answer they were looking for, and I was such a brat that I answered all the questions in what I considered to be that "jokey" manner. I never heard anything more about it until several years later when Mother confessed to me that they had let her know that I had scored one of the highest marks they had recorded. Apparently, she had talked it over with Dad and they had decided that I, being such a pain anyway, would become impossible if I knew of my potential.

Mother was a nurse and always loved the medical profession. I remember her sitting me down about this time and having a "serious talk" with me. This was alarming, as we never had serious talks. The gist of it was, "Why don't you think in terms of studying to become a doctor when you finish high school?"

I reeled. "You mean, cut people up and everything? You know that I wouldn't take biology in school because I wasn't about to cut up a frog. How much worse is it to cut up a person?"

There was a lot of talk about the nobility of the medical profession and the fact that doctors usually made lots of money — but to no avail. I put my foot down and said, "I'm doing music and languages and that's the end of it." My poor parents didn't have a chance. They didn't see the point in the language thing, and the idea of being able to make a living as a musician was unheard of. Music for them was for fun; nobody would pay you to do it. This music for fun attitude was a recurring thing during the first part of my career, and I've never ceased to fight against it. As for the languages, it certainly hadn't escaped my notice that most of the operas and a great deal of the song repertoire were in languages other than my own, and I determined to get at least a working knowledge of French, Italian, and German. I was, in effect, an autodidact. I certainly didn't learn much about French from the hopelessly inadequate course taught in high school in those days. My parents resigned themselves and, although of course I still had to go to school, there was no more talk of frogs and doctors.

I was in constant conflict at school. My schoolmates couldn't figure out this creepy guy who only lived for the time that he didn't have to be there. I was intensely focused on playing the piano, and all the rest — sports, dances, grades, everything else — either bored or enraged me.

Under the enraging category was definitely army cadets. The Second World War was at its most deadly and all the boys at school were forced to join either navy or army cadets. Navy was impossible because it involved evening training as well as marching around carrying a rifle after classes, which would have interfered with my piano practising. The time commitment for army cadets was confined to school hours. So, with high-strung resignation, I joined the army cadets and was given a revolting, ill-fitting, scratchy, totally unattractive uniform to wear and ordered to appear for training.

Of course, this was anathema to me for every reason. However, the summer before going into high school, I had had an accident with my bicycle and my eye had been pushed out of its socket by a blood clot behind the eyeball. It looked really creepy and I would revolt everyone by taking off my eye patch and glaring at them. With my eye looking like something from a horror film, I terrorized the principal of the school into getting me out of cadets until Christmas. When, after the holidays, I had to go back to cadet training, I noticed that when the roll call was read, my name was missing. My Grade B movie mind immediately went into full gear and I formed a plan.

Cadets were only called twice a week. On those days, after class, instead of reporting for duty, I would walk as casually as I could across the schoolyard and into the conservatory, where I would spend the time that I should have been at cadets practising the piano. As people were used to my not being at cadets because of my eye, I got away with it for three years.

As we all know, crime gets its comeuppance, and eventually I got caught. One day I noticed the vice-principal of the school looking at me narrowly as I was crossing the field. I got cold feet and began to run. At that very moment, I knew that the jig was up. The next day, inevitably, I

Here I am as a very unhappy army cadet, 1944. I think the uniform must have been made of iron filings, it was so itchy!

was called to the principal's office and asked for an explanation. My defiant denunciation of cadets, the school, and everything about it was not well received and I was ordered immediately to get into my horrid, scratchy uniform and report for duty. And what's more, as punishment for my three years of illegal freedom, I was given detention of two hours a day for the rest of my time in school. That meant that when everyone was released at four o'clock, I had to sit and do homework or whatever until six.

Maddening!

This gross injustice, which kept me away from my piano practice, climaxed at the preparations for "The Inspection," when some government creature came to pretend that we kids were a real military force, and we had to go through the farce of a military inspection. The man who was sent to prepare us for this essential bit of war effort was a sergeant from the regular army. I didn't really know the drill and I kept making mistakes — like dropping my rifle while trying to present arms. Of course, I did it on purpose because I hated the whole useless process. He was a little guy who looked like a tank, very, very butch. He screamed all the time.

There had been a movie with the comedy team of Abbott and Costello called *In the Army* in which they did a routine where Costello kept dropping his rifle while shouldering arms. I decided that if I were to stick to my guns (inaccurate metaphor under the circumstances) I had to do the Abbott and Costello thing. I dropped my rifle.

He screamed, "Pick it up!"

I snivelled, "Oh, golly, I'm so sorry."

"Don't say golly! Don't move! Stand there at attention!"

"But you said to pick up the rifle."

"Don't talk," he yelled. All the veins in his neck stood out. I was afraid that he was going to have a seizure. It was heaven.

He roared, "Pick up that rifle!"

"Pal, do you mean it or should I stand at attention?"

"Don't call me pal!"

"Oh, for heaven's sake, do you want me to pick up the rifle or don't you?"

The kids were all howling with laughter, but it was nerve-wracking because *au fond*, I'm a great coward when it comes to authority.

He shouted, "I'll show you one more time," and he did the three simple movements really snappily.

"Oh, sir," I said. "That was terrific!"

He became purple.

"You do it right this time or you're going to the Glass House!"

The Glass House was where, in the British Army, they put soldiers who proved to be intractable to discipline, in order to "break them," as they said. I'm not even sure that the Canadian Army had a Glass House, but I was sure that they weren't about to put a sixteen-year-old kid into it.

I picked the rifle up and thought, *This is a defining moment in my life. Am I going to have the courage to do what I think is right or not?*

I went through the motions and threw the rifle over my shoulder and exclaimed, "Oh, I'm so terribly sorry." I was immediately lugged off to detention again.

Now, when I recall this important moment of my youth, I'm of two minds about my smart-aleck behaviour. The poor man was only doing his job, but he had the misfortune to run up against my exaggerated sense of my individual worth as a human being. This tendency to go against the system has stayed with me. I've never been a joiner and I've managed to maintain my independent status throughout my career.

The principal of the conservatory in Regina was a man named Dan Cameron. He had been a singer, and when I told him that I was studying the piano so that I could be an accompanist for singers, he asked me to come to his studio. When I went in he had me sit at the piano. He put a copy of Handel's "Ombra mai fù," sometimes known as Handel's "Largo," on the stand and asked me to play it. The accompaniment for it is very easy but he sang it with a lot of exaggerated pushing and pulling of the tempo ("rubato" in musical terms). I knew that this wasn't the right way to do the aria, and I suspected he was doing it like that to test me somehow. I stuck with him like a leach, and when it was over he patted me on the shoulder and said, "It's not given to everyone to be an accompanist, but you will be one."

Martha Allan taught a class in accompanying at the conservatory and Mr. Cameron arranged for me to enroll. Almost immediately, I found that this was where I belonged. I had an innate sense of what the singers were going to do and I was instinctively supportive of them. Martha was marvellous at these classes. Her husband, who sang at the class along with several other singers, was a very good baritone. He sang everything from Broadway to oratorio and opera, with German *lied* and French *mélodie* as well. It was a great training ground for me; I got to play a terrific amount of repertoire and Martha's advice was invaluable.

One of the other students at the class was a beautiful and sensitive pianist who was much more advanced technically than I. Her name was Shirlemae Grain. We became pals, and Martha put us together doing two-piano repertoire. Shirlemae did first piano and I did second. We got along really well and were soon playing a lot of stuff together.

Inevitably, I suppose, I thought that I was falling in love with her. But, as I was so absorbed with music, and as she was rather skittish, I didn't really pursue it. I was too busy trying to keep up with her far superior technique and at the same time struggling with the horrors of school, so any true feelings of romance were shoved aside.

I finally graduated from high school, the happiest day of my life up to that point. Dad got a new job in Saskatoon, but it was decided that I would stay in Regina to continue working with Martha. Living quarters

Shirlemae in 1947. The lucky girl who got away.

were arranged with an old friend of my parents, a widow named Annie Hailstone. She was a charming Englishwoman who lived in a tiny basement apartment. I moved my piano into her living room and slept on the couch for a year.

I was very happy because I was out of school, away from home, and studying music full time. Mrs. Hailstone asked me what I liked to eat for lunch. I told her that my favourite food was tomato soup and lemon pie, and sure enough she served me tomato soup and lemon pie every day for nine solid months. For years afterward I couldn't look either one of them in the eye.

My lessons with Martha were very stimulating, although they were not very regular due to the fact that she was suffering from various health problems. She realized that I was working under a handicap because of my double-jointed fingers. (Later, Guerrero said that I had the worst fingers he'd ever worked with.) In order to try and strengthen them, she gave me a book of very strenuous exercises by a man named Pischna. Of course, I hated them; this wasn't what I wanted from music. I wanted to express something and I resented the time spent in trying to develop a technique.

But Martha insisted, so I would get up in the morning and do the mindless Pischna while looking at muscle magazines, and when I finished, instead of doing my Bach Prelude and Fugue, I would read through opera scores. I was already an opera freak. I had been caught by the Metropolitan Opera broadcasts at an early age. One day, twiddling with the dial of our radio, I had come across three singers singing their hearts out. I thought I had died and gone to heaven! It was the finale of Gounod's *Faust*. At the end, Milton Cross announced that the next week they would be broadcasting Wagner's *Tannhäuser*. At that time I had only the vaguest idea of Wagner ("The Wedding March"?), but when the overture started with the horns playing that superb melody, I started to cry. My father, a good man but none too sensitive, came into the room at that moment and said, "Oh, for god's sake, what's wrong with you now?" I didn't know how to tell him that I had just discovered my life's work.

At the conservatory, I envied everyone because they all seemed to know more than I did. However, although my technique was always weak, I had a real flair for accompanying singers. They seemed to sense that I loved them and that I realized my job was to help them look good.

The Saskatchewan Music Teachers' Association Festival was eagerly awaited each spring. The festival was a godsend as it gave us all a feeling that, through music, we were escaping, if only for a few days, the isolation that enveloped us all — at least from a cultural standpoint.

In order to attend the classes of the festival, I would play hooky from school (with or without my parents' consent; they finally gave in after I threatened to kill myself). I would be there from the earliest classes until late at night, listening to the singers and pianists. It was super because I got to hear all levels of performance and a wide variety of repertoire.

I was in my element, filling in my program with my idea of what mark a particular performance deserved. After a while, I got to be fairly accurate in my assessments, but I also developed a lifelong aversion to assigning numbers to a performance.

What is the difference between two performances of a Bach Prelude and Fugue that can be measured by 82 marks and, say, 84? Years later, when I was asked to judge competitions, I always balked at reducing artists to numbers. I've had to give way a couple of times, but much more often I've been able to convince the jurors to simply award the prizes to those whom the judging panel agreed were the most deserving. It's remarkable how little conflict develops when the issues are discussed instead of relying on a sort of numerical averaging. It also leaves the artists with a sense of dignity. Otherwise, they're left thinking, *Why did that person get 82 and I only got 81?*

The first time I entered the festival as a solo pianist was when Martha was off for the year having her baby. I don't think she would have let me play if I had been having lessons with her that year. She felt I wasn't ready, and she was probably right. The level of competition was especially high among the pianists. For instance, when I entered the Concert Class, where one was supposed to play two pieces from the concert repertoire, the other kids would play things like a Chopin nocturne with one of the big scherzos or ballads. The Concert Class was where all the little geniuses got to strut their stuff — and strut they did. I remember the girl who played before me did Liszt's "La Campanella" and Balakireff's "Islamay," two of the most technically demanding pieces in the repertoire.

When I got up to play after this fireworks display, I was so nervous that I could hardly get my hands on the keyboard, and the adjudicator very kindly asked if I would care to wipe off the keys before beginning. I didn't understand what he was talking about so I plunged right in. I was playing the Two Arabesques of Debussy, charming pieces but on an infinitely less demanding technical level than the repertoire that the other kids were playing.

The first one is a deliciously lyrical number and the second slightly more challenging technically. The first arabesque was my meat and I played it as if my life depended on it. The second one was not so hot, as my nerves gave out and I made a memory slip.

When the adjudicator got up to make his remarks, he said, "This has been an extraordinary class and there was one performance that lifted me right out of myself." Then he began his adjudications, leaving us all to wonder what the one performance was. He talked a lot about the remarkable level of technical ability displayed, but when he came to the arabesques he said, "These pieces don't in any way compare to the technical and musical demands of the other entries in the class, but, particularly in the first one, we heard the performance of an artist."

I barely heard what he said, and I was so dazzled that I didn't catch the reading out of the marks. I didn't win, but after the class the adjudicator said to me, "Your performance of the first arabesque moved me very deeply. If you work hard, you will make your mark in the world of music."

Of course, my head was in the clouds, but it was soon brought down to earth when I spoke to Martha about it. She said, "That's very nice, Stuart, but it's nothing new. We all know how musical you are, but the only part of his comments that you should pay attention to is 'if you work hard.' You have a long way to go before you 'make your mark.'"

This is the Prairie Lecture, as I called it, or "Don't get a swelled head." Mother gave it to me until the day she died. Nevertheless, the adjudicator's remarks gave a big boost to my confidence. Martha was right, of course. My whole career has been dogged by the fact that I never paid enough attention to the technical side of music. I was only interested in the sensual, colouristic qualities of the pieces I performed. I suppose that this was the reason for my attraction to French music. Oddly, I could play contrapuntal music very well, but it didn't interest me. At any rate, this shortcutting of my technique caused me a lot of trouble later on.

Martha had her baby and was delighted with her new role as mother. Unfortunately, this didn't leave her much time for teaching, and my lessons were again very erratic. I was very busy because it had got around that I was a good accompanist and I began to work as a vocal coach for singers, as well. There is a general lack of understanding of what the role of a vocal coach is as opposed to a singing teacher. Very broadly, a singing teacher builds the singer's technique and the vocal coach deals with matters of interpretation and languages. Of course, there are singing teachers who are also great interpreters and very knowledgeable linguists, but when a coach decides that he knows how to teach singing, things get very sticky. There are many examples that I know of where a coach will try to take over the singing teacher's role; the results are almost always negative. Naturally, when one has coached for sixty-five years, as I have, one picks up technical tricks that can be very helpful for a singer, but that's what they are, tricks, and they in no way substitute for a rigorous technical foundation. The problem can arise, as has happened with me several times, that a singer will be so pleased with the help I've been able to give them they begin to think of me as their singing teacher. I wish I had five bucks for every time I have said "I am not a singing teacher."

In spite of my irregular lessons with Martha, I learned the B-flat minor Nocturne and the A-major Polonaise of Chopin and Debussy's famous nocturne "Clair de Lune" for the 1948 Music Festival. In the lieder class, I played for a lovely soprano who sang Schumann's ravishing "Der Nussbaum." The Schumann song has one of the loveliest of all song accompaniments, and with its delicate whispering arpeggios and subtle weaving of the vocal and piano part, it was right up my alley. The adjudicator was wildly enthusiastic and we won by a big margin. I didn't win any of the piano classes, but my playing of the Debussy and the Chopin nocturne won high marks and very encouraging comments.

At the end of the festival, there was a competition for the most promising students in the piano, vocal, and violin departments. It was always a very exciting event and the public was fascinated. Also, there was a scholarship of $200 (a considerable amount in those days, enough to pay for a season of lessons) awarded to the winner.

Imagine my shock, terror, and dread when I was informed that I, playing the Chopin nocturne, was chosen to represent the piano division in the scholarship evening. Naturally, everyone was expecting that one of the virtuoso kids would be chosen. I don't know how I got through it, and when they announced that I was the winner, the audience went bananas. The rest is all a blur in my mind.

Martha was, as always, cool and reserved, although much later I heard from a mutual friend that she was as surprised as everyone else. I got the Prairie Lecture once again from Martha, but Mother refrained for some reason. However, that Stage-Mother stare began to flicker at the back of her eye. Fortunately, Dorothy was doing very well with her singing and so whatever designs Mother may have had slumbering *au fond* they were spent on Dorothy.

Martha then bowled me over with some advice: "I'm sorry that I haven't been able to give you the kind of preparation you need, but I feel that whatever there was for you in Regina, you have done. It's time for you to leave home and strike out on your own. But there's something I want you to remember. We are pioneers in this country when it comes to culture and that's not going to change in my lifetime, nor probably in yours." (Given the remarks made during the last few years by our highest government officials with regard to the arts in Canada, she was a prescient prophetess!)

After the end of the war, the boys in the services began to return to civilian life and, with the assistance of the Department of Veterans Affairs, they had money to spend on their education. The Toronto Conservatory of Music (TCM), soon to be called the Royal Conservatory, was where most people went to study music in Canada. I was dying to go and be part of this action and, after I had won the festival scholarship, there were great discussions about with whom I might study in Toronto.

After winning all her classes in the Vancouver Festival, Dorothy had gone to Halifax to study with Ernesto Vinci, a refugee from Nazi Germany. When he was engaged to teach at the conservatory in Toronto, Dorothy followed him there. In Toronto, she coached with a fellow who studied with Alberto Guerrero, a Chilean pianist who had settled in Toronto. In the way students have about their teachers, he told Dorothy that the *only* person to work with was Guerrero.

In the spring, the TCM sends people around the country to conduct exams for the degrees they offer. As a faculty member of the conservatory, Guerrero came to Regina in 1948. One of his ex-pupils was a friend of Dorothy Schmidt, Martha's assistant with whom I had worked while

Martha was off making her baby. Dorothy had a supper party for this pupil and she invited Guerrero, Martha, and me. When Guerrero heard that I would like to study with him, he asked me to play something. I played the Chopin nocturne, *very* slowly and *madly* sensitively, doing my best to sound serious and impressive. He allowed that it was very charming and that he would talk with Martha about my studying with him.

When we pressed him to play, he said, "I've been on this examination tour for over a month now and I haven't touched the keyboard in all that time, so I'll have to play something that doesn't take many fingers." He then proceeded to give a ravishingly beautiful performance of Chopin's Berceuse.

When he finished, I said, "If *that* doesn't take fingers, what do you play when you *have* fingers?" He smiled and shrugged. Of course, it was quite breathtaking and we were all enchanted.

The next day, Guerrero took me for lunch and we talked about music. I remember that he ordered sweetbreads. I thought that perhaps they were a variation of French toast. I asked him what they were and when he told me that they were usually made from the pancreas, I demurred. This was not tomato soup and lemon pie!

He was a great conversationalist. He asked me about the kind of music I liked. I told him that my ambition was to be an accompanist for singers. He said, "Ah, but to be an accompanist, you must play very well." He asked me if I liked opera. I told him that I spent most of my time playing through opera scores. When he asked what my favourite opera was, I immediately replied, "Debussy's *Pelléas et Mélisande.*"

He practically dropped his fork. "How do you know *Pelléas?*"

"I've heard it twice on the Metropolitan broadcasts and I fell in love with it. I can hardly wait to get a copy of the score."

"Do you know that *Pelléas* is *my* favourite opera? I named my daughter Mélisande in honour of the opera's heroine." (Much later, Mélisande told me that she hated the name *and* the opera.)

After the luncheon, Guerrero had a meeting with Martha. Then it was announced that Mr. Guerrero would indeed accept me as a pupil in September. I, of course, was thrilled. I felt rather badly about leaving Shirlemae and Dorothy Schmidt and my other pals, but those feelings were overwhelmed by the excitement I felt that my real life was about to begin.

Alberto Guerrero in 1937. He gave me this photo to remind me of the perfect hand position for playing the piano. Alas, my pudgy, stumpy little paws could never really manage it.

Chapter 2

My Life Begins

I came to Toronto in the summer of 1948 because the celebrated English (actually, he was born in Toronto, but lived most of his life in England) accompanist Gerald Moore was giving a three-week master class in accompanying at the conservatory. The plan was to take the course in July and then begin lessons with Guerrero in September.

For the first week, I lived with Dorothy and her husband, a man she had married the year before. He made no secret of the fact that he resented my intrusion on their life, so I went to live at the YMCA. The Y was conveniently located just a block from the conservatory (both buildings have since been torn down), and I began the class. I quickly realized that the Y was not where I wished to live, however. All those big butch guys with their sidelong glances gave me the willies. There was a registry of rooms for rent of which I availed myself, and I took a room in what was then the northern part of Toronto.

Moore turned out to be a totally charming man with an encyclopedic knowledge of the song repertoire. And he was funny. He had endless stories about the singers with whom he had worked, plus wonderfully detailed ideas about the songs on which we were working.

We all played something for him and then he assigned repertoire for each of us to study. For my piece I played the Ständchen of Strauss. It's a tricky piece, very light and fleet. I had fallen in love with it in Regina after I had heard it done in the lieder class at the festival.

I played it well and Moore was very complimentary. He then assigned me four songs from Schubert's song cycle, Die Schöne Müllerin. I've always loved Schubert, but I've never been able to play his music. It demands a kind of pianism that has never been my forte, constant repetition and too thick in the bass. Years later, in Vienna, I was allowed to play a piano from Schubert's time — around the 1820s — and I could see what he was about. The action on the pianos of his time was rather like the action on a pipe organ — very light and easy to play repeated notes. The modern grand piano has a much deeper action and it takes a lot more effort to play. Mind you, there are lots of pianists of our time who play Schubert superbly, but I was not one of them.

As a result, I failed to consolidate my first impression with Mr. Moore, and my subsequent appearances at the class were decidedly less successful than my initial one.

Nevertheless, those three weeks were a revelation for me. I was introduced to the enchanting world of Gabriel Fauré and Henri Duparc, and I'm still in their thrall. Moore's favourite songwriter was Schubert, so we had days that were totally dedicated to the problems of his songs. Moore had a wonderfully amusing and helpful trick of dealing with Schubert's Die Erlkönig — a notoriously difficult accompaniment with endless octave repetitions in triplets that wore me out after a few bars. His solution was to divide the octaves between the two hands, and when he did it, I defy anyone to tell that he wasn't doing it as written. Some people in the class were shocked at this "faking" of Schubert's intentions, but years later I read a quote from Schubert himself that said, "Let others play the triplets if they wish, they're too difficult for me!" (Schubert: A Critical Biography, by Maurice J.E. Brown. Da Capo Press, New York, 47.) Apparently, Schubert played the octaves as quarter notes instead of triplets; infinitely easier to manage.

As well as introducing me to a whole new world of music, I met at the class some of the people who were to be of primary importance to my later career, in particular the sopranos Lois Marshall and Elizabeth Benson Guy and the harpsichordist and lieder coach Greta Kraus. There was also a boy named John Coveart, a very accomplished pianist and already an important musician at the conservatory. When I told him that I was worried about having nothing to do in August, he suggested me for the job of music counsellor at a boys' summer camp in the Lake District north of Toronto.

I was of two minds about this. I really needed the money, but anything to do with organized sports or boys in general froze me with horror. It turned out that I wasn't wrong, because it was a ghastly experience.

I had been told that I was to play for an occasional recital and for the National Anthem and the camp song at breakfast. All well and good. What they didn't tell me was that if it rained, I was expected to play between meals to entertain the boys. The summer of 1948 turned out to be very rainy, so I was playing practically every day for three solid weeks. At the camp, the music staff consisted of two singers, a violinist, and a cellist. Thank heaven I was a good sight reader, but with the amount of music I was expected to read, I was pressed to the wall to keep up.

The strain soon began to tell. I got the flu and a terrible cold, so instead of wearing shorts like everyone else, I had to skulk around in long pants, an overcoat, and a hat. Shades of Glenn Gould! (I didn't even know Glenn at this point.)

I managed to alienate everyone. They had an expression at the camp that was used all the time as a term of admiration and that was "He's woodsy" — *woodsy* meaning someone who is comfortable living in the woods. I am not, and never have been an outdoors person. I like indoors. I definitely didn't fit into this "woodsy" environment. I was the misfit *par excellence*.

There was a guy at the camp, a psychology student, who was spending the summer taking everyone's IQ. He was aware of my outsider status and he was sympathetic and very kind. He took my IQ and said that he was very impressed. As he was the only person in the camp to whom I could relate, I was very grateful and began to rely on him for company. In all probability he hadn't expected this attachment, but I clung to his friendship like someone drowning.

On the final night before the camp broke up, I got wind of a plot that was being hatched to "get me" for being such a jerk all summer. I told my friend about it and he said, "Never mind about those thugs. Come and stay with me tonight in my cabin. We'll lock ourselves in and, short of them burning the cabin down, we'll frustrate their stupid plot."

My feelings of gratitude, combined with his insecurities about his sexuality made for an interesting night. The goons made an appearance, but discouraged by our barricade, soon went off. He and I discussed the possibility of becoming lovers, but his wavering and my total inexperience finally resulted in our falling asleep and nothing developing. The next day, I returned to Toronto and never saw him again.

I was supposed to start my lessons with Guerrero at the beginning of September, but I didn't hear from him. I wasn't sure how to proceed. What's more, I had to find a job. I don't know how they did it, but my parents had agreed to send me forty dollars a month to help keep me afloat. Although, of course, in those days, forty dollars was worth a lot more than it is today, it was not enough to pay the rent and feed myself.

An acquaintance suggested that I try to get a job as an usher at Eaton Auditorium, a beautiful Art Deco concert hall in downtown Toronto. I applied and was delighted when they told me that I could start immediately. They paid two dollars a night and I signed on for six nights of the week. Like everything else in Toronto in those days, they were closed on Sundays. Someone said of that time that there was only one thing to do in Toronto on a Sunday, but that there were hundreds of places in which to do it. The city was known as "the city of churches."

The job was a godsend. Every evening there was a concert and many evenings the concerts were by the greatest artists of the time. Eaton Auditorium was celebrated for its acoustics and for its knowledgeable and enthusiastic audiences. A typical season would include three or four series of concerts featuring the likes of opera stars Helen Traubel, Ezio Pinza, and Lily Pons, and pianists Vladimir Horowitz, Artur Rubinstein, and Rudolf Serkin: in other words, the elite of the musical world of the time.

As a music student I was early on called to turn pages for the accompanists of the singers and string players. One of my biggest thrills came when I turned for the celebrated American accompanist Dalton Baldwin. He was playing for the Belgian baritone Gérard Souzay. I noticed that before going on they would have little *sotto voce* conversations in the wings. At that time my French wasn't good enough to catch what they were saying, but I noticed when they began to perform that Baldwin was transposing most of the songs up or usually down. Transposing from one key to the other is something I've never learned to do. Some pianists can do it easily, but others like me never master it.

The recital went very well. Souzay was a very handsome man and very communicative. The ladies particularly adored him. When they got to the group of Duparc songs, I thought, *they certainly won't transpose these difficult and complicated songs.* But before going on they switched to English for their chat and I was astonished to hear Souzay say "Remember, L'invitation down a third, Lamento up a second, Manoir down a fourth, and Chanson Triste down a third." Then I watched thunderstruck as Baldwin played them all transposed at sight. Fifty years later, I met Baldwin and reminded him of the incident. I asked him if he could still do this and he laughed and said "Oh sure! It's just a trick."

It's a trick that would have saved me a lot of trouble during my career!

My very worst experience turning pages occurred at the Toronto debut concert of the famous German soprano Elisabeth Schwarzkopf. The week before, she had made her New York debut to ecstatic reviews and the auditorium was sold out, with seats even on the stage, which was never allowed.

As always, I was concerned about my part in this auspicious event. (Actually, if you can read music, there's not a big problem about turning pages, but I was very self-conscious about my contributions and nervous about meeting this big star.) What would she be like? Would she speak English? Would she speak to me?

The door of her dressing room opened and out flowed this dazzling creature in a flame-coloured dress with her classically beautiful features and shiny golden hair.

She said, "Hi. How are you?" I must say I was expecting something rather grander.

I said, "Miss Schwarzkopf, I'm so—"

"You're the page turner? Good. Are you a music student?" In perfect English, without a trace of accent, she promised, "We're going to have fun this evening and you'll have a good time."

Little did she know.

Arpad Sandor, the distinguished Hungarian pianist, was her accompanist. He was very nervous and seemed terrorized by her. Before they went on, all charm dropped away while she gave him instructions in the manner of a Panzer division general.

The first part of the program went beautifully. She was in great form and he played excellently. Just before intermission, she sang the two Cherubino arias from Mozart's *Le Nozze di Figaro*. The first one was charming. For the second one, Sandor opened the music and pointed out the fact that there were two copies of it. He said something that I didn't hear and he launched into the introduction. I had no idea what he had said, but I thought, having done a lot of accompanying myself by this point, he wanted to play the first page from the first copy and then switch to the second for the rest of the aria. I had myself occasionally done this to avoid an awkward page turn, so when they got to the bottom of the first page, I whisked the music smartly off the stand.

"No," he hissed in a strangled scream. He tried to get the music back onto the stand and of course it went flying all over the stage. In my shock and stupidity, I shoved right in front of him and pushed his hands off the keyboard, murmuring "Oh, I'm so terribly sorry."

The two of us went flying around the stage trying to get a hold of this piece of paper while Miss Schwarzkopf went bravely on, a capella. This clown of a page-turner and this poor wreck of an accompanist were clawing at the air, trying to catch this wayward piece of music while she sang all by herself.

Needless to say, the audience's attention was riveted on the two desperate acrobats and was not paying much attention to Madam and Mozart.

When we finally got the music back, Schwarzkopf looked at me as if she were planning my execution.

The rest of the program was more or less without incident until the last group. This section consisted of songs by Hugo Wolf, and it turned out that they were short ones printed on two pages only and so there was no turning necessary, but there I was anyway. The encores began. There were six of them and they, too, were all on two pages. I still had nothing to do. When they came to the last one, I said to myself, *This is really stupid, my going out there all the time for nothing. I'll stay in the wings for this last one.* They went out. There was a pause and a giggle from the audience. I looked out and there was Sandor beckoning and saying, "Get out here!" There was one page to turn. I skittered on and, of course, there was a storm of applause. I was as red as a beet.

When they finished, Schwarzkopf came over to me and said with a steely smile, "Now, I'd like this young man to take a bow."

I whined, "Oh, no."

She said, "Yes, yes my dear. Stand up and take a bow. Now!"

I stood up, embarrassed to death, bowed my head and took a step back. One of my friends said afterward, "For one ghastly moment, I thought you were going to curtsy."

Although I was having a great time at the auditorium and hanging out with the other kids at the cafeteria of the conservatory, I wasn't practising or having lessons. I couldn't figure out why I hadn't heard from Guerrero. When October arrived and I still had heard nothing, I decided to phone him. He said, "Why haven't you called me before? I was beginning to worry about you." For some reason, I had it in my mind that he would call me. At any rate, we set up a time for our first lesson and, very excited, I presented myself at the appointed time at his studio. He taught in a rooftop studio in his apartment rather than at the conservatory building. I never understood how he managed that, as all the other teachers were expected to teach at the conservatory itself. At any rate, his studio was very quiet and charming and it was certainly more comfortable than the spartan rooms at the "Con," as everyone called it.

I was very surprised when I went to the piano and noticed Guerrero lying down on the chesterfield. He said, "Play something." I was used to Martha, who sat right beside the keyboard and was ready to jump when anything went wrong, and here was Guerrero, languidly saying "Play something." After I got to know him, I realized that he, in his wisdom, saw that I was a nervous wreck and so he was doing what he could to calm me down.

"Should I play the Chopin nocturne?"

"No. You played that for me in Regina. Play something else."

"I could play 'Clair de Lune.'"

"Beautiful! I love Debussy."

I played the Debussy.

"That was excellent. Now play me some Beethoven."

"I don't have any Beethoven."

He sat up immediately.

"You've never played Beethoven? What about Bach?"

I gulped. "No Bach either."

"Well, what *have* you played?"

"I have the Chopin and the Debussy and a lot of songs."

"You have two pieces in your repertoire? Ah," he sighed. "I see that we have quite a bit of work to do."

In his admirable book, *Searching for Alberto Guerrero*, the celebrated Canadian composer John Beckwith gives a clear and penetrating analysis of Guerrero's life and his methods of teaching. More importantly, he redresses a grave injustice. Guerrero's most famous pupil was, of course, Glenn Gould. At the height of his fame, Glenn made some remarks about Guerrero that have been taken at face value by a number of Glenn's (mostly European) biographers. These authors knew neither Glenn nor Guerrero, and their conclusion — that Guerrero was an ineffectual teacher — is not only bad reporting, but manifestly unfair.

He very quickly saw that my musical abilities were not focused on the piano, per se. Thus, our lessons would often take the form of a discussion on, for instance, the relationship of Picasso to the French school of music composition in the first two decades of the twentieth century. I found these discussions profoundly stimulating and, no matter what the topic, Guerrero was always able toward the end of the lesson to bring the subject to bear in some form or another on the piece of music that I was supposedly there to study.

I hope that I haven't suggested that Guerrero was totally laissez-faire. He was simply a genius at discerning what each individual pupil was capable of absorbing.

One day, by mistake, I arrived for my lesson an hour early. Guerrero asked his pupil if she would mind if I sat in on her lesson. She readily agreed, so I went in and sat in the corner to listen.

The young woman was working on several of the Bach Sinfonias. I sat there astonished as Guerrero took her through all the intricacies of these Three-Part Inventions. His detailed analyses of the contrapuntal writing and of the various rules of ornamentation were crystal clear to even one like myself with very little interest in, or knowledge of, this style of music.

When it came time for my lesson I, in my brash and callow way, said to Guerrero, "Why don't you ever teach me like that?"

He replied with a twinkle in his eye, "I don't remember you ever bringing any Bach to work on. What did you bring today?"

"The Chopin G-minor Ballade."

"Fine," he said and proceeded to give me the lesson of a lifetime. His understanding and passion for this music was simply overwhelming. When, at the end of the lesson, I tried to tell him what I had felt, he simply said, "Work hard on what we've talked about today, and if you don't have time to practise, we'll talk about *Pelléas et Mélisande* next time."

Every few weeks, Guerrero would host a soirée where his most advanced pupils would perform the repertoire on which they were working. He invited me to attend, certainly not to play, as I was anything but advanced.

It was a great thrill for me as I heard excellent performances of a wide range of repertoire, and at the end, over refreshments; we would discuss the music that had been played. Guerrero was very much at the centre of these discussions, but he never dominated them. At the first couple of evenings, many of the students spoke of a remarkable young pianist who was scheduled to play at the next soirée. It turned out to be Glenn Gould, at that time sixteen years old.

Glenn was a rather retiring young man, charming and modest. He played a sonata by Carl Czerny. I had never heard anything by this incredibly prolific composer (his opus numbers go well beyond six hundred) except for a series of stultifyingly boring exercises that I had carefully avoided.

The sonata turned out to be very beautiful and Glenn played it superbly. At the discussion period afterward, I complimented him in my flowery fashion. He smiled and asked me what music I liked. When I told him that Debussy was my favourite, he said, "I don't like Debussy at all." In spite of this rather bumpy start, we became casual friends, and he and his parents were very kind to me for my first few years in Toronto. Glenn and I were too far apart in our temperaments and musical aims to ever form a close relationship. I wanted to emulate Guerrero's Mediterranean efforts to see things from all viewpoints and Glenn wanted concrete answers to everything. I remember Guerrero at one time gave us an exercise to do and suggested we do it ten times a day. I did it a few times and then forgot about it. Glenn came to his next lesson with it perfectly under control. He told Guerrero that he had done it a hundred times a day.

At that time, the Royal Conservatory, as it was now known, gave exams in ten grades. I decided to take the grade ten exam. I managed to get first-class honours in spite of the fact that my playing of the solo pieces was only adequate. Once the hurdle of the exam was passed, I couldn't find a job. The auditorium was closed for the summer months, so my parents suggested I come back to Saskatoon. Mother, who was nursing at the Saskatoon General Hospital, got me a job there as a porter. In spite of my lack of enthusiasm for the medical profession, I found that I really enjoyed working at the hospital. It certainly wasn't very demanding, taking patients from their rooms to the X-ray or physiotherapy departments and back. At the physiotherapy department, there were two young women technicians from Australia who were working their way around the world. We became pals, and one evening I invited them to come to my parents' apartment for a musical soirée. Mother and Dad had lived for several years in Saskatoon at that point, so they invited some of their friends, as well.

Dad suffered from angina toward the end of his life. He wasn't feeling well that evening, so he stayed in his bedroom with the door open, in order to hear the music.

I had been coaching a couple of singers in Saskatoon that summer who sang several pieces about which I gave some background information. (I've always had a facility for speaking to audiences and this was one of the first manifestations of a lifelong trait on my part.)

The evening was going along very well, when, from the bedroom there came a cavernous voice intoning, "Okay, when do we get a solo from the Big Man from Toronto?" Everyone thought this was very amusing. I found it less so, as the music I was working on that summer was Schumann's *Carnaval*, and it was certainly not ready for public airing. I played the easy parts not too badly, but it certainly wasn't a brilliant display and I could tell that Dad wasn't impressed. There were no more soirées for the Big Man from Toronto.

When Dad expressed reservations about my going back to continue my studies in the fall, I desperately did all I could to convince him that I wasn't in Toronto to become a great solo pianist, but that I was studying so that I could do what I knew I could be a success at — being a vocal coach. This concept was a hard sell for my parents, but I explained to them that I had begun to establish a reputation as a coach and that I was sure that during the next season I would be able to generate enough income from my work with singers that they could dispense with my forty-dollar-a-month allowance. Dad could never understand how anyone could ever make a living without a regular paycheque, but I was adamant and he finally gave in. Triumphant, I returned to Toronto in September.

I was, of course, thrilled to be back and to be studying with Guerrero again. The problem was that I didn't have a place to practise. I worked at various places around town and, when they were available, which was very rare, at studios at the conservatory. The conservatory was humming with activity and studios were very difficult to come by. Finally, in desperation, I begged my parents to send me our old piano from the Regina days. I think they were glad to be rid of it. No one played it anymore and their apartment in Saskatoon was really too small to accommodate it. Dorothy persuaded her husband to have it in their house as long as I used it only while he was at work.

Trying to be a serious musician in Toronto in 1950 — that eyebrow!

This worked for about a year and a half and then Dorothy and her family moved out to the suburbs and I had to find a studio. By this time, I was making enough at my vocal coaching to allow me to rent a room at the Hambourg Conservatory of Music in downtown Toronto.

The Hambourg Conservatory was located at the corner of Wellesley and Sherbourne streets in what was then midtown Toronto. It was housed in an old mansion that by 1950, when I took a studio, had definitely seen better days. There were lots of ancient looking photos on the walls (the building had been occupied by the conservatory since 1913) and it looked as if no one had dusted since then. (It has since been torn down.) However, I moved my piano into a small room there and was very happy. At last I had a studio of my own where I could practise and do my coaching.

I had started coaching singers in Regina when I was fourteen. I was good at it, and word soon got around in Toronto, so it wasn't long before I had a lot of students. The first place I taught was at an old church on Carlton Avenue opposite the Odeon Cinema. (Both buildings have since been torn down.) I coached a few people in the basement of that church. One of them, a girl named Victoria Bodner, had come from Regina. She was studying with Dr. Vinci. "Vinci," as everyone called him, had been very kind to me and continued to send me many of his pupils for coaching. Victoria did a recital at the conservatory that season and she asked me to play. This was my debut recital in Toronto. It went well and I continued doing concerts for the next fifty years.

Interestingly enough, about five years ago a girl came for a lesson and she introduced herself by saying that I had coached her grandmother. I said smugly, "Oh, no, my dear, that wouldn't be possible." But of course it was. She was Victoria's granddaughter!

One day a girl came to coach Violetta's first-act aria from Verdi's *La Traviata*. She said that she didn't really like the aria but that a producer had asked her to learn it and sing it for him because he thought it would suit her. I had always loved the piece and I had never thought much about it, but this was a challenge, so we got down to work.

Singing the aria at an audition presents a problem right from the start. In a performance of the opera, Violetta dismisses her guests after a long party. The orchestra plays busy and rather noisy exit music for the chorus and then, in the silence that follows, Violetta begins her recitative. The question for an audition is what to play to get her going. The exit music has nothing to do with what she is about to say, but to play a bald chord just to give the singer the pitch doesn't really work either. Whatever is used to get going, the singer has to take time to show us that she is thinking out loud rather than reacting to what's just happened in the orchestra.

Her first words are *È strano, è strano* ("It's strange, it's strange"). Verdi sets these two exclamations differently. The first *È* is marked as an eighth note and the second as a sixteenth. Also, the second phrase is on a higher pitch than the first. Obviously, he wanted two different approaches to these phrases. They shouldn't be sung with exactly the same expression and the most evident way to do this is to make the second phrase more emphatic either by singing it louder or, more subtly, softer. She goes on to exclaim that the words that Alfredo, her young admirer, has said to her are engraved on her heart. Verdi marks a crescendo on this phrase, and most singers sing it too loudly so that it breaks the contemplative mood. The phrase should start softly and then get louder as Violetta expresses her surprise. The next phrase is "Would it be a misfortune for me to have a serious love affair?" She has, of course, had many love affairs. After all, as a courtesan, that's how she makes her living. But to have a love affair that was not based on a monetary transaction would be something entirely new for her. This phrase is difficult to pitch properly with its tricky chromaticism at the word *sventura* ("misfortune") and then the whole tone at *serio* ("serious"). Many singers get out of tune at this point, but if they motivate the difference between "misfortune" and "serious" the tuning is almost always solved.

Her next phrase — "No man has ever caused that (a serious love affair) to happen for me. Oh, happiness which I have never experienced" — is set by Verdi with a great vocal flourish that is self-explanatory, but it is followed immediately by a very tender phrase when she says "to be loved and to love in return." This, of course, has to be an entirely different vocal colour from the brilliant phrase that preceded it. The power of the next phrase happens almost automatically as Verdi sets it in the upper range: "And can I ignore this offer of love, for the empty folly of my existence?" But on the word *my*, Verdi asks for a decrescendo on a musical turn, which magically suggests Violetta's despair at her empty life.

And this is just the recitative, before she even begins the aria! The world of opera is filled with these sorts of musical passages that reveal everything about the character of the person the singer is portraying. From the earliest period of opera there is a stunning example of this in Octavia's aria in Monteverdi's *L'incoronazione di Poppea* ("Addio Roma") and it continues through such examples as Susanna's "Deh, vieni non tardar" from Mozart's *Le Nozze di Figaro*, Isolde's Narrative and Curse, Manon's entrance aria, and Mimi's "Mi chiamano Mimi" among a host of others.

I was asked at one time to give a lecture on what it is to be a vocal coach and I chose Violetta's aria as my subject. The lecture lasted two and a half hours with an intermission. After intermission, a lady was heard to remark, "It's nice, but I don't know that I really want to go up to this level of comprehension." Of course, she was right. The audience doesn't need to know all this, but the singer must be aware of it if she is to give a convincing performance. Birgit Nilsson once replied to an interviewer who asked her about the difficulty of the high C near the beginning of Strauss's *Elektra*: "Sure, it's a tough note, but the audience hasn't paid to hear about my problems. They want to hear how close I can get to what Strauss wanted to say about Elektra at that moment."

At any rate, the girl got the job and has gone on to sing many highly successful performances of Violetta.

Guerrero decided that, having successfully passed my grade ten exam with the Royal Conservatory, I should attempt the Associate Degree. The requirements for this are considerably more demanding than for the grade ten. I really wasn't much interested in the piano, as such, but Guerrero convinced me that it would be advantageous for me to have the degree. I wanted to get it over quickly, so I stood for the exam in February instead of waiting until June. It was stupid of me. I wasn't ready and, although I passed, I was "conditioned" in pieces and technique, which meant that I had to do the exam again in June. I passed with first-class honours in June, but the setback in February upset my parents and once again they suggested that I come home and go to university to learn an honourable profession and be sensible. Being "sensible" has never been part of my makeup, and once again I refused.

It was a very exciting time for me. I was beginning to establish myself as both a coach and as an accompanist. But then I made two big mistakes.

The first was that, having achieved my degree in piano, I thought that this was enough and that I could now concentrate on doing what I wanted, which was, of course, to teach and play for "my singers." Partly because of that (as if having a degree meant anything in the performance world!) I decided that I didn't need to study with Guerrero any longer and that, because I didn't care about working on piano literature, I could concentrate on the vocal repertoire, which was what I really loved.

Guerrero and I remained great friends and I continued to visit his soirées, but to my later chagrin I stopped my lessons.

The second mistake I made related to "my singers." That possessive *my* is the villain here. Because I was bursting with ideas that seemed to work and because the singers responded so enthusiastically to what I had to say, I made the mistake of thinking that I should take over the direction of their lives and careers (shades of Svengali). At first all went well, but it wasn't long before I discovered that this proprietary behaviour was exhausting for me and eventually resented by the singers. Finally, realizing that my methods were being decidedly counterproductive, I learned to back off, partly from my own experience and partly because of what Guerrero once told me. He said, "You know, teaching is essentially simply exposing the pupil to what you think you know. After that, it's all up to the individual student what he/she does with the information you have given them." Of course, he was right, but it took me a long time and a lot of effort and struggle with myself before I was able to implement his advice.

By that time I was very busy coaching. At first, most of my pupils were singers whom I had known in Regina and who had come to Toronto to continue their studies. Chief among them was the soprano June Kowalchuk. June had one of the most ravishingly beautiful voices that I've ever encountered. Joined to this was an innate musicality that made all her performances truly memorable.

The Opera School at the conservatory quickly developed into a fully incorporated Opera Company. They presented their first season at the Royal Alexandra Theatre in the spring of 1950. The repertoire consisted of *Rigoletto*, *La Bohême*, and *Don Giovanni*. I heard through the grapevine that the girl who was to sing the role of Gilda in *Rigoletto* had become pregnant and had to withdraw from the cast. June knew the aria "Caro Nome" from the opera, so I told her to go and sing it for

Herman Geiger-Torel, the artistic director of the company, and Nicholas Goldschmidt, the conductor. She did, and they told her that if she could learn the role in a week, they would give it to her.

We spent every waking moment of the next week learning that part. It's a long role, but June had a fabulous ear and by the time she sang it for them, she knew it.

When the season opened, there was June as the first leading lady of what eventually became the Canadian Opera Company (COC). She had great success and went on to win the two big competitions on the CBC at the time: *Singing Stars of Tomorrow* in Toronto and *Nos Futures Étoiles* in Montreal.

The next season, June sang the title role in *Madama Butterfly* and then she asked me to go on a concert tour as her accompanist through the smaller centres of Saskatchewan and Alberta.

In Foam Lake, Saskatchewan, after an exhausting train trip, we were greeted at the station with banners, the mayor, and about half the population of the town. The mayor gave a nice welcome speech and then surprised us with a question: "Miss Kowalchuk, what colour is your gown for the concert?"

June, thinking they wanted to coordinate the presentation bouquet, replied, "It's gold-coloured."

The next day, we went to rehearse in the hall and they had painted the hall purple, presumably to compliment her dress! We were choking from the paint fumes, but it was a charming gesture anyway.

The day after the concert we had a long train trip to our next destination, Red Deer, Alberta. By this time we'd been "on the road" for several weeks and were both tired. On the train, a kid in the next row to ours was eating an orange. The scent from the orange was very powerful and June became more and more uncomfortable. She finally excused herself and went to the washroom. When she returned, she was deathly pale. I asked her if she was all right and she snapped back, "Of course, I'm all right! What's the matter with you?"

She was getting very cranky, so I backed off and we continued the trip in silence. When we finally arrived in Red Deer, we just had time to eat dinner before the concert. At the restaurant, June ordered a steak and she insisted that I have one as well. At that time, I wasn't very fond of steak and I told her so.

"You mean that I've been buying you steaks on this trip and you don't even like them?" she barked. "For god's sake."

This got my back up. June was from a Ukrainian family. She spoke the language at home, but she didn't really have a thorough knowledge of it. She was singing a couple of Ukrainian songs on her program. I didn't know Ukrainian, but I had taken notes when she coached the songs with a Ukrainian speaker.

I barked back at her. "Actually, you're pronouncing the word *hrud* wrong."

"What are you talking about?"

"You're pronouncing the word *hrud* incorrectly."

"I am not!"

"You are so! You're pronouncing it with a hard *d* and it's supposed to be soft."

"You're trying to tell me how to speak my own language? You don't know a single thing about Ukrainian."

"I remember that the word was pronounced with a soft *d*. You are pronouncing it wrong, and what's more, I hate steak!"

With that, the fight was on. We were shouting, and it must have sounded like we were about to kill one another. The whole restaurant was riveted. When we got to the hall for the concert, it was jammed to the doors; apparently, it had got around town that these two weirdoes who were obviously at each other's throats were actually going on stage to try to do a recital together. Everyone wanted to be there to see the blood flow. In the event, we disappointed them and gave one of our best performances.

The tour was in March of 1952. It turned out that June was pregnant with her first child. She didn't tell me about it until later. If I had known, I might have been a little more understanding of her moods.

Our last concert was a radio broadcast for the CBC in Winnipeg. Dad had been moved to Winnipeg from Saskatoon the previous year. I had lunch with him the day of the broadcast and I was shocked by his frailty. He had great trouble formulating his thoughts. We had lunch at one of those diners where you made out your own bill, but after trying several times he had to have me do it. The broadcast that night went well and when I called him afterward he told me that he was proud of me. We had never communicated very well and he was always skeptical of my ability to make a living as a musician, so I found this remark to be profoundly moving. That was the last time I spoke with him.

The next month, my brother Doug was killed in the war in Korea. The year before he had married a beautiful girl and was, I think, happy for the first time in his life. He and I had finally buried the hatchet and were beginning to develop a real friendship.

Two months later, Dad died of a cerebral hemorrhage. He had just turned fifty-four.

Chapter 3

Two Magnificent Teachers

I'm neurotic about being happy. I hate being unhappy with all its attendant tensions and anxieties. I had been very unhappy in Regina. I had very few friends, I wasn't a joiner, I didn't like popular music, and I was a protogay. Worst of all was the fact that no one would leave me alone to study my music. I was desperately trying to be something that I didn't have time to be. Certainly I wasn't much in Toronto, but at least I was working at what I wanted and not what someone else wanted or demanded I be — like a doctor, or an army cadet.

Many people have asked me if it was difficult to be gay in Toronto in the fifties and sixties. I suppose it was: I don't think it's ever easy to be gay. The point is that for me it was more or less a non-issue. I never had the nerve to pretend that I wasn't gay; I assumed that everyone knew. I was never secure enough in my belief in my musical background to risk spending what emotional energy I had having a relationship. I certainly wasn't confrontational about it, but I wasn't in denial either. I was doing what I felt was my role in life and although I thought at the time that I would have liked to have a relationship, I realize now that the fact that I didn't left me with the energy to pursue my life in music. I was happy. My pupils found me to be relaxed (in an admittedly high-strung way) and supportive and stronger than many people. I had an inner strength and I knew my own worth. I've been a success as a teacher because both the pupils and I recognized that strength. I was aware of it right from the beginning and now that I was using that recognition I was happy, and I've been happy ever since. (Not to sound like Pollyanna, there was a five-year interlude where I wasn't ecstatic. All in good time.)

Eventually, the Hambourg Conservatory ran out of steam and I had to find another studio. (The building has since been torn down.) There were three old mansions on Bloor Street and Mt. Pleasant Road that were collectively called the Wakunda Centre. The middle building of the three had four little rooms on the third floor that were rented out as studios. There was an ex-tenor in one and a lady with an uncertain past in another. The third one was occupied by a piano teacher who played a rather large part in my future life. She was a fascinating girl who smoked constantly; she always had a cigarette dangling from her lips. That was not so uncommon in those days, although I never smoked myself.

The rent was very cheap for a reason. There was a restaurant of some sort on the first floor. The people who ran it were decidedly shady types and none too hygienic. The place was overrun with rats. When you went to put out the garbage, you had to throw stones at the rats to chase them from the garbage pails. Eventually, I got tired of fighting with the rodents and I called the Health Department. They came up, took one look, and closed the restaurant. Needless to say, I wasn't very popular with the restaurateurs, but they slithered off into the night and were never seen again.

When Father died in 1952, Mother suggested that she come to Toronto with Patsy in tow and keep house for me. Having just achieved my independence, I was not happy with the idea of going back to Mama. Fortunately, Doug's young widow, who lived in Barrie, a small city north of Toronto, invited Mother and Pat to come there. There was a good hospital and a position available for an obstetrical nurse, so it was decided that the two ladies would move to Barrie. Mother loved the hospital, and Pat was happy at the school, so it all worked out well. And I was free to continue my Bohemian existence, or what passed for a Bohemian existence in Toronto in the fifties.

Soon we received notice that the Wakunda buildings were to be torn down. The cigarette lady decided that we should find a house and divide it into studios. Sure enough she found a small house near the Bloor and Yonge intersection in the centre of town. She knew a German dressmaker who needed a cheaper room in which to work, and she and I divided the other two rooms between us. There was still the room at the back of the house to let. We put an ad in the paper and it rented immediately, so we were all set. At least, so we thought.

The renter said her name was Mae Kerr. She paid in advance and moved in the next week. She put up a sign on her door that read MAE KERR, EXCULSIVE [SIC] DRAPERIES. She told us that she made draperies for the CBC television station. The day after she moved in there was a ring at the front door and there stood a worker in rubber hip boots.

"Is Mae here?"

"Well, yes, that's her door at the end of the hall."

He clomped down the hall. Mae let him in. He was there for about twenty minutes and then left. There were four other guys working on the street and they all went to see Mae, presumably to get their drapes done.

I said to the cigarette lady, "This is awful. Mae is running a whorehouse in there. You have to talk to her. I don't have the nerve."

The cigarette lady, with much more aplomb that I could ever have managed, explained to Mae that while we didn't condemn her profession, she had children coming to take piano lessons and we didn't want to risk trouble with the police. Mae asked if she could leave her stuff there for the rest of the month and moved out the next day.

Next, we rented the room to a social worker who promptly had an abortion there. Things were certainly colourful at that house. I introduced the cig lady to Glenn Gould and they immediately started an affair. I happened to walk in on them in flagrante one time and, of course, immediately backed out and rushed upstairs to my room.

Glenn was superb. After an appropriate interval, he knocked on my door. I invited him in and he immediately launched into a detailed discussion of Mahler's "Das Lied von der Erde." Very enlightening.

The house was great for making music, but it was a big pain as far as the heating was concerned. There was an ancient coal-burning furnace that worked most of the time. The problem was, coal makes for a lot of ashes and the furnace was in what wasn't a proper basement, but simply a hole in the ground with a ladder for access. Getting a bucket of ashes that weighed three thousand tons straight up a ladder required more muscles than I had at the time, but it had to be done. So, I bought myself a set of weights and began building my physique. Mr. Universe has nothing to worry about, but I'm still, fifty-some-odd years on, exercising regularly. I think this has contributed to my remarkably good health over the years. Now that I'm in my eighties, it's sort of a race to see which will come first — death or muscles.

During this period, I fell in love with two women who had a great influence on my musical development, Emmy Heim and Greta Kraus. Both ladies were from Vienna, both were Jewish and had come to Canada as refugees from the Nazi regime. Emmy was an elegant, frail, and charming woman. She had at one time been a singer, although when I knew her that time had long past. She was a tremendous aficionado of German song (lieder) and I got to know her because I offered to play for her lieder class at the conservatory. It was a volunteer job, but it was worth a fortune to me because I became exposed to this endlessly profound and beautiful branch of the singers' art.

Emmy had a passionate love for lieder and she could impart that love to her pupils in an indelible way. Schubert, Schumann, Hugo Wolf, and Mahler were her gods and she served them as a true devotee. Interestingly, Brahms and Strauss didn't attract her so much. She felt that Brahms didn't pay enough attention to the prosody of the language and that Strauss wrote for opera singers. Nevertheless, I heard her give some revelatory lessons on both those composers.

I adored Emmy. She called me her *böses kind* (literally "bad child," but more idiomatically "bad boy") because, although she told me she loved my enthusiasm, I played too many wrong notes.

I used to play for her private singing lessons as well as for her class. One time her pupil didn't show up, so she said, "Never mind. Let's sing something ourselves." There was a volume of Mahler songs on the piano. She said, "Let's try one of these."

She chose a song called "Wer hat dies' Liedlein erdacht?" ("Who thought up this little song?") I had played the song fairly often and I loved it. Although I'm not a fan of folk music, this song, which is not really a folk song, certainly sounds like one. It transcends the folk song idiom thanks to the wit and charm of Mahler's conception. From the very first words — *Dort oben am Berg* ("Over there on the mountain") — Emmy had me in raptures. Not that her voice was anything much anymore, but this music was in her bones. I've never played anything so well in my life; I looked at her afterward and she said with a twinkle in her eye, "Not bad, eh?"

Not bad indeed.

She told me lots of wonderful stories about her life in Europe. She worshipped the legendary French *diseuse* Yvette Guilbert and was determined to study with her. This unhandsome woman would mesmerize her audiences with endless verses of watery French waltzes — in her hands, according to Emmy, every verse was a tremendous drama.

Emmy tracked her idol down one time in London, England. She managed to get an appointment to meet her at her hotel. Emmy told me that she was almost dead from fright, but that the old woman received her very politely.

"Do you have talent, Mademoiselle?" she asked the quaking Emmy.

"I ... I hope so, Madame," Emmy stammered.

"*Très bien.* Come back in three days and say the phrase '*Prenez place, Madame*' [sit down, Madame] forty-five different ways and then we shall see."

Emmy never went back.

Emmy died in the mid-fifties after a long and very difficult battle with cancer, but she was really indomitable to the end. Because I had had the experience of helping patients at the hospital in Saskatoon, I was able to help her get from her bed to the sofa in the living room where she received her pupils. As her condition worsened, some of her friends rented a hospital bed, which was set up next to the piano. She continued teaching from there. At the last lesson I played for her, her pupil was singing Schubert's song "Erlafsee" (Lake Erlaf); it's one of Schubert's most elegant and gentle creations. Emmy had visited this small lake in Austria many times. (The lake is actually called Erlaufsee, although Mayrhofer, the poet, called it Erlafsee, and that's how Schubert set it.) She brought all her recollections and her love for Schubert to a passionate elucidation of the song.

· After the pupil left, I kissed Emmy for what we both probably realized would be the last time, and she said, "Try to play the right notes, Stuart."

The first piece I played for Greta Kraus was Schubert's "Der Tod und das Mädchen" ("Death and the Maiden"). One of Schubert's most famous songs, it is a dialogue between the two title characters. There is a slow, solemn introduction (Death), a fast, agitated section (the Maiden), and then a beautiful series of phrases for Death and a reprise of the piano introduction. I played the intro as slowly and solemnly as I could. Greta looked at me narrowly and said quietly, "What does *mässig* mean?" (The expression mark at the beginning of the piece is *mässig*).

I made a dive for it. "It means massive, heavy."

"Nein!" (She suddenly sounded as if she'd been studying diction with Hitler.) "It does *not* mean massive and heavy. It means moderately. *Moderately!* How do you expect to play lieder if you don't know anything about German? Get yourself a German–English dictionary. Look things up. No wonder you're playing so ridiculously slowly. You didn't know what the word meant. It means moderately. Now, get going. Play it faster!"

That was my introduction to Greta.

As might be gathered from the above, Greta was a passionate musician. Near the end of her life she told me, "When I can't play the piano any more, I don't want to live." And she didn't.

Emmy was a singer. Greta was a keyboard artist. She played the harpsichord and she was for many years the only professional harpsichordist in Canada. I adored playing for her class and I came to realize that her banshee outbursts were simply her desire to get as close as possible to what the composer wanted.

For years I dreamt of her virtually every night. In my dreams she was always yelling at me for some outrage that I had perpetrated against Brahms or Mozart or whoever. When I finally told her about these dreams, she was horrified. Once, she and her husband had a New Year's Eve party. At midnight she gave me a huge kiss and said, "With this kiss, I exorcize myself from your dreams." I felt like Brünnhilde at the end of *Die Walküre.* Come to think of it, she probably would have made a great Wotan. The crazy thing is that the kiss worked. I almost never dreamt of her again.

I learned a tremendous amount from Greta, but then I had a tremendous amount *to* learn. At her class she was constantly challenging me about the meaning of words that I didn't know. I mean, it takes a while to read through the dictionary!

"What does *leidenschaftlich* mean?" she would yell. I was stupid enough to keep trying to guess.

"Something to do with the body?"

"Nein."

I was thinking of *leib*, the body. Of course, *leidenschaftlich* means "passionately."

Sigh.

Eventually I learned something, and Greta and I became great pals. I turned her pages when she played harpsichord continuo for the Bach Passions with the Toronto Symphony under the inspired direction of Sir Ernest MacMillan. Along the way she formed a baroque ensemble and I would turn for her rehearsals and performances of this at that time unfamiliar repertoire. One day she asked me to learn the orchestral reduction of the harpsichord concerto by the Swiss composer Frank Martin so that she could practise with me for an engagement with the CBC Symphony. I found working on this (then) new piece to be challenging and exciting and our rehearsals were terrific. She worked like a demon.

One evening we started at five o'clock in the afternoon. By eight I was beginning to fade.

"I suppose you're hungry."

"Uh, well—"

"Come with me."

In the kitchen, she opened the refrigerator door. Talk about "the cupboard was bare." There was nothing in it but two hard-boiled eggs. She handed one to me along with the saltcellar and said, "Let's eat." She ate her egg and I ate mine and it was back to work until eleven o'clock.

Many years later, Lois Marshall invited me to a party. However, she neglected to tell me that it was to celebrate Greta's eightieth birthday. I don't know how that happened, as everyone else arrived with gifts for Greta. Mortified, I improvised.

"Greta, for your birthday I will take you for a glamorous dinner, and before I will come to you and play the Mozart sonata that I'm currently working on."

"I can't think of anything I'd rather have," she cried.

On the day agreed upon I arrived at her home at 5:30 p.m. The sonata takes about twenty minutes to play, so I made the reservation for supper at seven, thinking that would give us plenty of time. Forget it. At nine o'clock we were still discussing the third movement. I said, "Darling, this is fabulous, but I'm going to have to call the restaurant."

"What for?"

"We're supposed to be having supper, remember?"

"Oh, well — if we must."

At the restaurant, she barely glanced at the elaborate menu, and said to the waiter, "A double scotch and some fish."

Some fish turned out to be the most expensive thing on the menu, and I watched in dismay as she pushed it around her plate, eating at most three mouthfuls. Never mind, all through the meal she regaled me with the most wonderful stories of her life in Vienna in the twenties when she had her studio above the offices of Freud's daughter Anna, and when she would go every night to the Vienna State Opera to hear Richard Strauss conduct performance after performance of his own operas. This, of course, was a long way from Regina.

She had a great story about Yvette Guilbert. Apparently, Emmy wasn't the only girl in Vienna in love with the famous *diseuse*. Greta told me that she went to all her concerts and one time she ran up to the stage at the end with a lot of other kids, to be closer to her idol. Guilbert came out to take a bow. Greta told me, "At that time I had masses of bright red hair, which I wore in braids. When Guilbert saw me, she leaned over, put her hands on my head, and said '*Quels cheveux!*' I didn't wash my hair for six weeks after."

When, after having paid a small fortune for supper, I took her home, she gave me a huge kiss and said, "Stuart, the meal was very nice, but working on the Mozart was divine."

On a memorial broadcast for Greta, who died in 1998, Canadian composer John Beckwith movingly remembered women like Emmy and Greta as the last generation for whom music was a temple rather than a supermarket.

Chapter 4

Two Magnificent Singers

In Regina, in the spring of 1948, I wrote a letter that changed my life. There was, on CBC Radio, a nationwide competition called *Singing Stars of Tomorrow*. This was the competition that June Kowalchuk won several years later. It was a very popular show, with singers coming from all across Canada. Besides the high-level exposure, the program offered several very lucrative prizes. My sister Dorothy sang on the program several times. While she was studying in Halifax with Dr. Vinci, she met a girl from a small town in Nova Scotia — Bridgewater. She wrote home that this was a girl to watch and that she would be performing on *Singing Stars* the next week.

Her name was Elizabeth Benson Guy. For her aria, she sang *Aida*'s third act, "Oh, Patria Mia." This is a very treacherous piece with a notoriously difficult approach to a high C near the end. Elizabeth nailed it. I was particularly impressed because, shortly before, the Metropolitan Opera had broadcast *Aida*, and the soprano, who was later announced as being indisposed, had cracked very badly as she attempted the high C.

I wrote to Elizabeth (she was forever after known to all her pals as Libby), congratulating her on her performance and introducing myself as Dorothy's brother. She wrote back thanking me and saying that Dorothy had told her that I was hoping to come to Toronto in the fall, and if I did that I should look her up. As it happened, Libby took Gerald Moore's class and I met her there.

The CBC began to broadcast performances of operas in 1948 and Libby was their favourite diva. One day I met her and her husband in a supermarket and she told me that she was going to sing Puccini's *Turandot* for the CBC that fall. I had the nerve to say, "I love *Turandot*. Could I come and play for one of your rehearsals?"

She agreed, and that was the beginning of a twenty-year professional association and a lifelong friendship.

She was a lyric soprano and should never have sung *Turandot*, but she had a rock-solid technique and a perfect voice for radio, so she got away (and with distinction) with singing much heavier repertoire than she would have sung in an opera house.

In their nine seasons of broadcasting, the CBC Opera engaged Libby for about twenty roles — everything from Mozart's Fiordiligi in *Così Fan Tutte* (in a repeat performance, they lost their Dorabella at the last moment. There was another soprano available for Fiordiligi, so Libby switched roles and sang Dorabella) to Violetta in Verdi's *La Traviata*, to Tosca in Puccini's opera to Tatyana in Tchaikovsky's *Eugene Onegin* among others. I helped her learn them all, a tremendous experience.

Libby was a terrific musician with a wonderfully instinctive understanding of a great variety of repertoire. She was Greta Kraus's daughter-in-law and sang cantatas by Buxtehude and Schütz and Bach with Greta's baroque ensemble. With the CBC Symphony she sang Berlioz's "Les Nuits d'Été," Mozart's C-minor Mass, Mahler's Fourth Symphony, the Chansons de Ronsard of Milhaud and, most beautifully, the final scene from Strauss's *Capriccio*, among many others.

This was heady stuff for me, but the most wonderful thing about working with Libby was the recital repertoire for which she was in great demand. She sang German like it was her native language and under my influence she became a superb interpreter of my favourite songs by Debussy, Fauré, Chausson, and Duparc.

One time she was engaged to do a recital for the CBC. She had done many already, but they were mostly German lieder. She knocked me out by asking me to play for this upcoming recital. She was not one to respond to overt emotion and when I practically slobbered in trying to thank her, I thought for a minute I had blown it and that she would change her mind. My fears were unfounded, but I learned to be less explosive in my dealings with her. Her program consisted of a group of songs by the respected British-Canadian composer Healey Willan and (I expect the reason I was asked to play) a group of French songs, her first for the CBC. "Clair de Lune," a gorgeous setting of Verlaine's famous poem by a man named Josef Szulc (does anyone know of anything else by this obscure composer?), Debussy's "Chevaux de Bois," Duparc's fabulous "Phydilé," and Paladilhe's (who?) adorable "Psyché."

Libby sang the program beautifully and I played well. It was the beginning of many recitals that I played on the CBC. Many of these were for her. There is a tape of one of them in the library of the Faculty of Music at the University of Toronto in which she sings the most beautiful performance of Fauré's Cinq Mélodies de Venise that you're ever likely to hear. The only problem is that I played a wrong note at the end of the first song in the group, "Mandoline." *Groan!* In those days, everything was live to air — no going back to fix things. Alas! I was never famous for my right notes.

Fortunately for me, all this took a great deal of preparation and so I worked with Libby three and four times a week. Like me, she was a morning person, so I would present myself at the huge, gloomy mansion that she shared with her husband John, their two children, her mother-in-law Greta Kraus, and Greta's husband Erwin, John's father. Usually, Greta would meet me at the door.

"Good morning, Stuart. Have you figured out what *mässig* means? Heh, heh, heh!"

After which I'd make my way down to the basement where Libby had her studio. Libby was a very hard worker and there was no saving her voice; she always sang full out. She was very serious about her work and I loved our sessions together.

There are in every performer's career several concerts during which everything falls into place and everything that you hope to achieve somehow occurs. One never knows when it will happen, and it can be maddening in that it doesn't seem to be something that you can will into life. I had one of the most perfect experiences of my life as an accompanist playing for Libby at McMaster University in Hamilton, Ontario. I thought, as the program was going along, *What is this? Libby is singing beautifully,* but that wasn't unusual. What *was* unusual was that I couldn't seem to do anything wrong and everything I attempted came effortlessly and seemed to inspire her to give a great performance. At the end of the recital, Libby and I looked at one another and we *knew.*

Driving home, we hardly spoke a word, but when she dropped me off at my home, she said, "Why doesn't that happen every time?"

I shrugged and said, "Who knows? Let's just take our cookies when they're passed."

Several years later, a musician whose opinion I respected told me that he had been at that concert and had recognized what was happening. He said he was so moved that he couldn't come back stage after, but that the memory of the experience would stay with him for the rest of his life. Mine too.

Libby was, like many artists, basically a shy person, and it wasn't easy to get her respect, but once I managed that, we became great friends as well as enthusiastic colleagues. She was a great cook, and she fed me a lot. I used to drive her crazy by telling her that I loved eating at her place because she served good, plain food. One time she served tapioca pudding for dessert. I demurred, saying that we never ate it at home because my sister Dorothy had turned up her nose when Mother tried to serve it. When asked why, she had replied that she wasn't going to eat pimple pudding. I became a hero to Libby's two kids because they never had to eat the unspeakable pudding again.

In 1957 the CBC stopped producing operas for radio. The last production was Janáček's Jenůfa. As Libby was the diva of the series, the honour of the title role went to her. However, Jenůfa has, in effect, two leading ladies. The other role is that of Jenůfa's stepmother, the Kostelnička. Libby's role requires a strong lyric soprano, ideal for her, and the Kostelnička demands a great singer-actress, a dramatic soprano. This role was given to a newcomer from the United States who had recently moved to Toronto with her Canadian husband. The CBC certainly got their money's worth. Her name was Mary Simmons.

Simmons had already done a blazing performance of Puccini's Turandot for the CBC, but it was only during the rehearsals of Jenůfa that I was introduced to her by Libby. Apparently, she asked Libby about me and Libby told her that I was her coach. Mary contacted me and we hit it off right away. Because of her great musicianship and her magnificent voice, she was very much in demand, and we plunged into working on her engagements.

Working with Mary was like trying to work with a whirlwind. As always with these great artists, it wasn't easy to gain her confidence, but once that was established the relationship was tremendous.

Mary was a fantastic musician. She had trained as a violinist, and like many string players she was obsessed with intonation. I doubt if such complicated pieces as Alban Berg's concert aria "Der Wein" or Schönberg's big orchestral songs or his Second String Quartet, to say nothing of Milhaud's crazy "Machines Agricoles," where the singer sings in a different key from the accompaniment, were ever done as accurately as when Mary sang them. When I met her she was already a celebrated lieder singer. Anyone who has sung the great German song repertoire knows of the importance of the texts and their relationship to the music. Mary's German diction was idiomatic and she sang the work of all the famous lieder composers. Through our work on the French repertoire, where I was able to convince her of the import of the declamation and the importance of colour, she was able to become as great an interpreter of French repertoire as she already was of the German.

One time she was engaged to sing excerpts from Berlioz's opera *Les Troyens*. She arrived for rehearsal as always, perfectly prepared. For whatever reason the rehearsal was scheduled on the afternoon of the performance, but there, at the rehearsal, she experienced every singer's nightmare. The orchestra plays an unfamiliar introduction, the conductor looks at the singer, and nothing happens. The librarian of the orchestra had neglected to send Mary the first five, very tricky pages of the recitative that precedes the aria. After a flurry of explanations and apologies, Mary, who was not one to be put down, announced that she would learn the recitative in her dressing room and would perform it an hour later at the concert. She then sang and no one was aware that she had learned the passage moments before the performance.

One of Mary's great successes was Schubert's tremendous cycle of twenty-four songs, Die Winterreise. These overwhelming songs have never appealed to me. My problem with them is that twenty-four shades of gloom are too much gloom for me. Mary sang them at least once a season and she would always rehearse them meticulously. She performed them with the well-known American pianist Leonard Shure. One time, he wasn't available for a concert in Cleveland. As I had rehearsed them many times with Mary over the years, she asked me to play for her. I was aghast. As I have already indicated, I've never considered myself to be a Schubert pianist and I certainly had never contemplated performing Die Winterreise. However, Mary was very persuasive, so I settled down to practise. I dreaded the concert because, although I worked like a dog on the songs, I knew that I was nowhere near where Mary was. I felt that I was letting down both her and Schubert. Fortunately, the concert was cancelled and the next time she was engaged for the cycle Leonard was available, so I was spared.

Mary was wonderful to work with for many reasons and one of the best was her terrific sense of humour. One summer day when the temperature and humidity were as nasty as only they can be in Toronto, we were working on Schubert's enchanting song for soprano and piano with clarinet obbligato, "Der Hirt auf dem Felsen." There is one awkward leap up to a high B and Mary was having trouble with it. She did it again and again. We were sweltering and nothing I suggested seemed to work. The phone rang. I answered it, and when I came back to the studio, there was Mary, having taken off all her outer garments, sitting in her lingerie.

"Mary, your underwear is very pretty. Now, put your clothes back on."

"No. It's too hot!"

"Mary!"

By this time we were both roaring with laughter, and after she'd got back into her clothes we tried the passage again, and out came the high B like a jewel.

She had sung Die Winterreise with great success at the festival organized by Rudolf Serkin at Marlborough, Vermont. They asked her back to do a recital in their winter series and she asked me to play for her.

She had a mortal fear of flying, so her husband, Jack Bernstein, a high-powered businessman in the film industry, agreed to drive us to Vermont in his big Cadillac. When we got to the New York throughway, surely the longest, straightest, and most boring highway in the world, Jack put the pedal to the floor and we zoomed right along.

It was a Saturday afternoon and the Metropolitan Opera was broadcasting Strauss's *Elektra*. I had brought my score and we were happily enjoying all the racket (*Elektra* is very noisy) when I glanced out the window and was startled to see a police car driven by an officer who looked as if he was about to suffer a stroke as he made frantic gestures for us to pull over. I pointed out this apparition to Jack and we duly stopped.

The officer leaped out of his car and came storming over to ours — his face was actually purple. He screamed, "I have been following you people for fifty miles with all my sirens going and my lights flashing and it's taken all this time to catch up with you. Get out of the car! (Nowadays, they say "Please get out of the car," but this was a long time ago.)

Jack was a big bear of a man and he was very cool about it all, but Mary was something else. She had sung Puccini's *Tosca* and as far as she was concerned her husband was the incarnation of the opera's Cavaradossi, and the officer (Officer Sbardella, as it turned out) was the evil Baron Scarpia, head of the Roman secret police who was about to victimize poor old Jack. She lunged at the glove compartment and, drawing out a long screwdriver, shot out of her door and in full cry made for Officer Sbardella. At that point, because I remembered that in the opera Tosca stabs the Baron to death (mind you, with an elegant dining knife instead of a screwdriver), I felt something had to be done. So I managed to intercept her and, after a fair amount of yelling and wrestling, things calmed down. Jack was given a ticket and we were allowed to proceed.

As we were getting back in the car, the officer said to Jack, "I don't know what your wife does, but she sure has a healthy pair of lungs!"

As you can gather, Mary was all fire and intensity. This, of course, carried into her performances and the audiences loved her. The concert in Vermont went really well. For her lieder group, Mary sang the Dichterliebe cycle of Schumann. Schumann was much more my meat than Schubert, so I was in my element.

For an encore, Mary sang the aria "Pleurez, pleurez mes yeux" from Massenet's *Le Cid*. This great piece, in which Massenet captures some of the grandeur of the French classical theatre of Corneille and Racine, was a battle-horse for Mary, and the audience exploded with applause at the end. Afterward, a little old French-Canadian gentleman grasped Mary's hand and said, with tears in his eyes, *"Oh, Madame, Pleurez mes yeux. Pleurez mes yeux."* He couldn't finish the sentence and Mary always said that she was never sure whether he liked it or not.

On the way home, I said to Jack and Mary, "If we run into Officer Sbardella again, I'm heading out across the fields." Fortunately, we missed him, but coming down the mountains from Vermont we hit a patch of ice and the car slid perilously close to a ravine. We were never in any real danger, but as we got back into the car and Jack eased it back onto the highway, Mary, who as a young girl had been an actress in the Yiddish theatre in Philadelphia, said. "Oi! Dis is a trip?"

Chapter 5

A Final Lesson

By the mid-1950s I was playing a lot of concerts for the CBC and many recitals for kids at the conservatory. I was, of course, delighted to be busy, but there was a down side. I was so busy learning repertoire that I didn't have any time for practising. The result was inevitable. My playing, never immaculate, got more and more approximate and, although I was generally admired for my musicianship and sensitivity to the singers, the feeling was that it was time that I acquired a more reliable technique. The final blow came when Arnold Walter, the head of the Senior School of the Conservatory, began to suggest to the singing teachers that they encourage their pupils to use someone else as their accompanist.

I asked Guerrero if he would take me back as a pupil. When we discussed my problems, he said, "Stuart. You are never going to be a great technician. You started studying too late and your hand isn't ideally suited to playing the piano. However, if you're willing to work hard, I can certainly give you things that will allow you to play with more confidence. These lessons will, in all probability, not be so interesting for you musically, but eventually they will give you the freedom you need."

He was not one for technical exercises for their own sake. He always worked through the problems in the music itself. He assigned me the Two- and Three-Part Inventions of Bach. These wonderful pieces were actually a lot of fun to practise and the counterpoint was very satisfying to work out. The problem for me was that, although I could certainly recognize the magnificence of the conception of Bach, I was, and continue to be, attracted to music written between the Napoleonic Wars and the First World War.

I worked with Guerrero for the two years before he died in 1959. He was right, of course, in that the lessons, while never dry, were not as much fun as the ones I had taken with him originally. Nevertheless, I realized how foolish I had been in not taking advantage of the amazing resource he was. Whatever success I had in my playing career I owed to those two years with Guerrero.

Guerrero didn't try to restrict me to the seventeenth century. That was not his style at all. He knew that I had a particular knack for Debussy and Ravel, and he was amazingly revelatory about the French school. There was a little competition at the conservatory where you played a selection of pieces by Debussy or Ravel and he suggested that I try for it. I was thrilled that he would send me up for what was really an event for advanced pianists. When I played my program for him, he merely said, "You will be one of the more interesting ones."

In the event, there were many more accomplished people in the competition and the prize went to someone else. Nevertheless, the experience had done me a world of good and I learned a terrific amount about getting around the keyboard from the work that I did to prepare for it.

I was chronically short of money. The CBC at that time had a talent program on television called *Pick the Stars*. I didn't have a television set, but friends told me about the show. I saw it a couple of times and decided to audition for it. I played "Clair de Lune" (what else?), and was accepted.

The trick about the show was that there were three judges across the country and each one had a vote, but the studio audience would have two votes, measured by the applause meter. When I played, none of the judges voted for me, but I had packed the studio with my pals and they made a tremendous racket at the end of my piece, so I got the studio vote. The judges split their votes between the other competitors, so I won and was asked to play again the next week.

Easy.

The next week I played "Malagueña" by Lecuona, a very popular piece at the time. It was easy and flashy — just the thing for television. This time, one judge voted for me and, of course, I had my studio full of goons, which meant I had three votes.

Nothing to it.

The problem was finding something to play for the next week. I really didn't have anything suitable, so I threw together a Chopin waltz. This was not the thing with which to win a competition. The judges divided their votes between three of the other competitors and I had my usual pals. When I finished playing, they went into their routine and the applause meter went over the top, but then, for no apparent reason, as my claque was screaming, it immediately dropped down. Years later, I asked the producer of the show what had happened and he admitted, "We had to get rid of you. It was becoming too obvious what was going on."

Fair enough.

I had appeared three times, by hook or by crook, and I was richer by three fat fees. However, I received a phone call a couple of weeks later telling me that I would be expected to appear on the grand finale, as everyone who had been on the show more than twice was supposed to play or sing something with the orchestra. I was in a quandary, because I'd never worked on any concertos. I went to Guerrero and frantically asked him what I could possibly learn from the concerto repertoire in the few weeks before the final show. He immediately suggested the finale of the Variations Symphoniques by César Frank. It's an adorable work and I'd always loved it, so I worked night and day and by show time it was more or less ready to play.

For the telecast — live, of course, in those days everything was live — I was in one studio and the orchestra in another. They sent the sound of the orchestra into my studio and at the rehearsal the amplifiers didn't work and I got hopelessly lost. Naturally, my nerves were shot. There was a big drum roll. The orchestra played the introduction, while I sat at the piano dressed by the costume department in a set of white tails. I looked like a teenaged whale. The lighting was dim so that I was seen in silhouette, but when I started to play, a huge spotlight placed at the end of the piano came on and totally blinded me. The rest is a blur, but Guerrero said after that he thought it had been quite good.

The other competitors included Teresa Stratas and Paul Anka, so I had scant hope of winning the grand prize. But when, at the end of the show, they made the announcement, they said that the standard of competitors was so high — *blah blah blah* — that they had decided to give us all first prize.

Hurrah!

The summer was always a slow time for coaching, so with the money from *Pick the Stars* I decided to spend July and August practising. By about the middle of August, I went up to Mother's cottage on Lake Simcoe for a few days. While I was there, I contacted Guerrero at his summer place a few miles along the lake and asked him if he would give me a lesson on the material on which I had been working. He replied that he would be delighted, so one beautiful day I went along to his place.

I took him an enormous bouquet of flowers and at his door I sang out "Alberto, Alberto, Alberto," and from within, he sang back "Son qui," just like Tosca's entrance in Puccini's opera. I gave him the flowers and we began working. We worked on Chopin's F-minor Ballade and Debussy's suite of piano pieces called Estampes. We had worked for well over two hours when his wife came in and said, "You gentlemen have worked long enough. Here are some refreshments."

That lesson could have gone on forever as far as I was concerned. Among the myriad details that we discussed, one particular one stands out in my memory. Guerrero was, of course, being from Chile, a Spanish speaker, and his playing of Spanish music had a particular air of authenticity. The second of the Debussy pieces is his hauntingly beautiful evocation of an evening in a southern Spanish town, "La Soirée dans Grenade." He praised my playing of this ravishing piece, but then he said, "Remember, Stuart, that in Spanish music, even in pseudo-Spanish music like this, in the background, there is always The Knife." That immediately put the finger on what was lacking in my performance, the rhythmic intensity so subtly realized by Debussy.

This was only one of the stunningly apposite things he said that afternoon that has remained in my mind as a glowing beacon my entire life.

Guerrero was taken ill that September and died quite suddenly in early October.

Death is always annoying. This great man was seventy-three years old, he had an encyclopedic knowledge of music and a revelatory ability to transmit this wisdom, and there it was — gone. It still seems to me to be a profoundly stupid waste.

After Guerrero died, I was at something of a standstill. My coaching was picking up again but I felt that I needed something extra to keep my development happening. I played a recital at the Art Gallery of Toronto that was successful enough to encourage me to try something more ambitious.

The Music Library of Toronto was presenting a girl chained to the piano doing all the sonatas of Beethoven. I went to one of her concerts and got an idea. I approached the lady who ran the library and said, "Would you be interested in celebrating the one hundredth anniversary of Debussy's birth, due in 1962, with a series of concerts of all his piano music and all of the songs?" (I shudder now to think of my boldness, or foolishness, or whatever one might want to call such an enormous proposition, especially from someone of my limited experience.)

The lady allowed as how they would be very interested and how many concerts did I think it might take to do this. "About seven," I answered airily.

"Very well," she replied, and I was on.

I have always felt that the music of Debussy spoke to me with greater force than that of any other composer. I still feel that way almost fifty years later. Originally, it was just a gut feeling, although I now realize that it was part of a general reaction to French art that has followed me all my life. No musician would deny the profound and beautiful effect of German music, nor, I would hope, the brilliant and exhilarating thrill of Italian opera, but for me the balance achieved by the French between the thoughtful depths of German art and the more immediate éclat and exuberance of the Italian genius was the deciding factor in my espousal of all things French.

I think the first piece of Debussy's that I played was "The Little Shepherd" from the Children's Corner Suite. I had since studied many more of his works, the two books of Images and the Estampes, some of the Préludes, and a number of the early compositions. It didn't take me long to realize how much more there was to learn. When I looked through the Études, I realized that I was in way over my depth.

I went back to the lady and whined that I didn't think I could handle the Études. She was at first unsympathetic but fate intervened in the form of a message from the head of the library saying that they couldn't fit seven concerts into the schedule for 1962 and that the most they could manage was five. So I was off the hook. In the event, I played three piano concerts and two song recitals. I managed the first book of the Études, the 24

Préludes, the two books of Images, the Estampes, the Suite Bergamasque (including my old warhorse "Clair de Lune"), the Children's Corner Suite, and various bits and pieces. I asked Shirley (she had dropped the Mae) to come from Regina and play the Petite Suite for piano duet. She and Martha came for the second concert where I had programmed the suite and she played as expertly as always. Afterward, I regretted not asking her to play the Suite Pour le Piano, which was one of her party pieces and which I hadn't programmed, but by the time I thought of it the programs were printed and the library ladies discouraged the idea.

For the two vocal concerts, I engaged two of my coaching friends, Ruth Rashkis and Joy Alexander. Ruth had come to work with me on the advice of her psychiatrist who had felt that making music would prove to be of benefit to her mental health. And it was. Ruth was a beautiful woman with a good voice and a vibrant intelligence. We worked together several times a week for about ten years, and during that time she covered a very large part of the vocal repertoire. Joy, a lifelong friend, sang the second song recital.

When Joy went to New York to study, I would sometimes visit her there and play for her lessons with the Croatian soprano Vera Schwarz. Schwarz, a very glamorous woman, had been a diva at the Vienna State Opera in the twenties and early thirties. She had sung in the early performances of Richard Strauss's *Die ägyptische Helena* and Strauss would often play for her recitals. Once, Joy sang Strauss's Ständchen at her lesson, and when it was over, Schwarz said to me, "Stuart, Strauss himself played that song for me many times, and you played it much better than he did."

I came back to Toronto all puffed up with this compliment, but when I told Greta Kraus about it she said, "I should hope you would play it better than Strauss. He was a terrible pianist."

I have since talked with a number of people who heard Strauss play and it seems that he wasn't such a terrible pianist. He simply didn't like to practise.

All in all, the Debussy series was a success and an invaluable experience for me musically; but in order to prepare it, I had had to stop teaching and concentrate on practising. As a result, I was flat broke at the end of it. A short job playing for the summer class of Herman Geiger-Torel, the artistic director of the Canadian Opera Company, had shown us both that we were of opposite temperaments and we parted company, not to work together again for many years.

By the fall, things were desperate. For the one and only time in my life, I had to borrow money to pay my rent. Fortunately, I had recently made what was to be a lifetime friend — the writer and broadcaster Dodi Robb. She lived in an apartment upstairs from mine and she generously lent me the money for September. However, I couldn't rely on this stopgap. Something had to be done.

The *deus ex machina* (or rather the *dea ex machina*) appeared in the form of my old pal June Kowalchuk. She had recovered her health from the problems that had forced her to give up her career ten years before. She was living in Hamilton, a steel company city about forty miles south-west of Toronto, and she had started an opera company there. She had programmed *The Merry Widow* for a November production and she needed someone to prepare the chorus. Could I spare the time to go to Hamilton once a week for rehearsals?

Could I?

I had never prepared a chorus before, but I found it to be rather easy. The steelworkers and their wives and sweethearts turned out to be very enthusiastic, the show was a success, and the Hamilton Opera Company was launched. I was offered the job of coach and rehearsal pianist. What's more, the Hamilton Conservatory of Music was looking for a singing teacher. I applied for that job and got it. I was a "singing teacher" in name only. They didn't have a category for vocal coaching. At any rate, I passed myself off as a singing teacher, I got a large class going almost immediately, and my financial problems were more or less solved.

As soon as my bank account would stand it, I became a leather freak. I was already halfway there as I had bought my first pair of leather pants in 1960, before my financial collapse after the Debussy series. This purchase elicited a combination of consternation and hilarity among my friends. "Isn't it amazing what they can do with Saran Wrap these days?" was a typical reaction.

Never mind. I was happy and I've never looked back. There have been more horses and cows go through my closet than you could find at the Calgary Stampede. Someone remarked that it looked like an abattoir in there. Recently, when I wore a copy (in leather) of a German uniform to teach a class at the University of Toronto, one of the students remarked that I looked like a Nazi.

I replied "Listen, kid. The Nazis were vulgar and disgusting people, but they had great tailors."

Some people seem to think that if you're "into leather," you must go to interesting meetings where people with chains and tattoos explore the darker side of Krafft-Ebing. This was never the case with me. I like it, that's all. Sometimes a cow is just a cow.

The last word on the subject was given by the distinguished American music critic Martin Bernheimer when we were both appearing on the *Metropolitan Opera Quiz* broadcast a few years ago. There were some murmurs about my outré outfit — leather jodhpurs and riding boots. "Oh, leave him alone," said Martin. "It's the national costume of Canada."

Chapter 6

Two Audacious Recitals

I settled into a routine of taking the bus to Hamilton once a week. At first this involved travelling on Tuesday afternoons, teaching at the conservatory, grabbing something to eat, and then doing the rehearsal for the opera company. But I soon had more pupils than I could manage, so in order to accommodate the new ones, I would leave Toronto Tuesday mornings, teach all afternoon, do the rehearsal, stay at the YMCA, then teach all day Wednesday before staggering back onto the bus and homeward.

All this was great for my bank account, but it turned out to be hard on my soul. The problem was that in those days music-making in Hamilton was strictly an amateur business. I've fought all my life to have music taken seriously as a profession, but do what I might with master classes, lecture recitals, an opera workshop, or what have you, I could never raise people out of the idea that music was just a recreation. This eventually began to get me down.

I got so that I dreaded Tuesdays. I would glumly get on the bus, spend two days pushing the stone up the hill like Sisyphus, crawl back to Toronto on the bus, and go to my favourite restaurant, La Scala (since torn down). There I would celebrate having the rest of the week to myself by knocking back more booze than was good for me. The next Tuesday I would go back to Hamilton and, sure enough, the stone had rolled back down the hill.

One time, I had scheduled a lecture recital on the songs of Duparc. I was having supper at the Connaught Hotel before the concert, and when I looked across the room, there sat my mentor of fifteen years earlier, Gerald Moore. I went over and introduced myself as having been one of his students at the accompanying class he had given in Toronto. He was polite enough to say that he remembered me and explained that he was in Hamilton to give one of his celebrated lecture demonstrations the next day. When he heard that I was giving my Duparc recital that evening he immediately said that he wanted to come. His wife, however, demurred, saying that they had been travelling a great deal and that Mr. Moore needed an early evening.

I expressed my regrets at not being able to come to his talk, as I had appointments in Toronto the next day. Moore then said an amazing thing.

"What is someone of your talent doing in a backwater like Hamilton?"

I spluttered.

He continued. "I remember your playing very well. You should come to England. I could introduce you to many people and you would be very busy."

I was astonished. I had no money and couldn't possibly go to England. I was straining every nerve end to make enough to keep myself together, and the idea of taking off for Europe under any circumstances was totally out of the question.

I went and gave my Duparc lecture to twelve people and began to brood. Having to work in Hamilton with a group of people who would never take music seriously was bad enough, but to have someone of international stature like Moore suggest that I could be successful in London, and not be able to take advantage of his kindness, sent me into an untypical fit of depression. To cap the climax, a week or so later I played for a girl who was auditioning for Seiji Ozawa, at that time the musical director of the Toronto Symphony. After the audition, he asked to speak to me. He said, "That was extraordinarily beautiful. Why haven't I heard you before?"

Again, splutters. I have no facility in dealing with the Mighty. He went on, "The Fauré was as beautifully played as I've ever heard it. You must play more often." This incident absolutely put the nail in the coffin as far as I was concerned. I had to get on the bus for Hamilton right after the audition. On the way, I pondered the remark made by President Lyndon Johnson of the United States that the greatest tragedy for any man was not to be used to his full capacity. I thought, "Lyndon, you are talking to me."

Obviously, if I weren't to stagnate, something had to be done. After tossing around several projects, I finally decided on doing a major recital.

But where? Hamilton was certainly a dead end. Toronto had never really taken me seriously as a pianist. The next step had to be New York.

Because I had never conceived of myself as a solo pianist (all I ever really wanted was to be an accompanist for singers), the idea of a New York recital had never entered my mind. But, at this point, I needed something to jog me out of the mediocrity in which I was stuck. There was no question that I was playing much better than I had when I came to Toronto, but it was highly questionable as to whether I had the technical equipment, let alone the musical ability, to pull off a major event like this.

This was 1964. I gave myself two years to prepare. I continued with my coaching in Toronto and my work in Hamilton. This was going to be an expensive proposition and I had to make as much money as I could before jumping off the end of the world.

I got off on the wrong foot in that I chose a program totally unsuited to my abilities — Rachmaninov, Liszt, Ravel — pieces that I loved, but pieces for which I simply hadn't the technique to do justice. I tried the program out at several places and it was clear to me that it wasn't ever going to work. I had to retrace my steps. I had lost nearly a year attempting this repertoire. Nineteen-sixty-seven was Canada's Centennial celebration for the independence of the country and everyone had a Centennial project dealing with some aspect of Canadian life and/or culture. I decided that my Centennial project would be my New York debut. I had had to postpone my project for a year, so 1967 fitted the bill.

A surprise phone call from Glenn Gould resulted in my getting back on track. I hadn't seen Glenn for about ten years. Our paths had diverged, he became famous and I didn't. We had lost touch.

He said, "I hear you're planning a recital and I want you to play it for me." I replied that I had recently changed my repertoire and that nothing was really ready but that I could give him an idea of where I was, from the pianistic standpoint, at the moment. He said, "Fine, next week I'm playing with the New York Philharmonic. I'm coming home right after the last concert, so come and see me after that." We made the appointment, and I showed up at his apartment.

As soon as I went in, Glenn said, "Listen to this." With that, he put on a tape. He had played the Brahms D-minor Concerto with Leonard Bernstein the week before and Bernstein had announced to the audience that he didn't agree with Glenn's interpretation of the piece but that Glenn had been incredibly persuasive. He said that the only other time he'd ever done this was when he last worked with Glenn. Then, they had performed the concerto slower than anyone had ever heard it.

Of course, it *was* very slow, but Glenn always had enormous charisma and a tremendously convincing way of presenting himself under every circumstance. One thing that had enraged Glenn about the critics of his performance was the comment that he had played the piece that slowly because he couldn't manage the notorious double octave passage in the first movement. This was, of course, nonsense, as Glenn's technique was the equivalent of any of the great pianists. When the octave passage came, it was hair-raising, and it certainly wasn't that slow. Glenn never did anything arbitrarily. He played the concerto at that speed because he felt that over the years, virtuoso pianists had jacked up the tempo in order to show off their techniques. I personally doubt that Brahms would have wanted his work to be played *that* slowly, but that was Glenn.

He finally said, "Oh, yes. You're here to play, aren't you?" After listening to this thunderous performance of the Brahms, I wasn't about to skitter through my little Liszt numbers, so I played the F-minor Ballade of Chopin. It went okay, but it was careful. When I finished, he said, "Well, you're certainly playing better, but you still play like an accompanist. What else are you playing?" When I told him, he snorted, "That's stupid! You can't play that kind of thing. You don't have the technique. Choose something else less technically demanding. If you try to play that repertoire, the critics will devour you." This was, of course, precisely the conclusion to which I had already come. He then got up and said, "Let me look at your music."

He took the copy of the Chopin Ballades and read through the A-flat one. It was superb. I accused him of having practised it but he denied it, saying, "No, I've never looked at it before but I've heard it all too often. It's such a boring piece."

I remonstrated with him. "But it wasn't at all boring! It was magnificent. You should play Chopin."

"Oh, no. This music doesn't speak to me at all."

Later, he did make a recording of Chopin's B-minor Sonata, but he did it just to prove that he could. As far as I know, he never programmed any Chopin. I mentioned something about Guerrero, and he said casually,

"I never learned anything from Guerrero." Glenn was very authoritative about everything and he hated to be contradicted, but this gross injustice infuriated me.

I said, "Glenn that's totally untrue! Every time I watch you play, it's like having a lesson with Guerrero. You do everything exactly the way he tried to get us all to play." He shrugged and said mildly, "Is that so?" and the subject was dropped.

Glenn's advice, though rather roughly put, was undoubtedly the correct one, so I *did* change my repertoire. One of the great experiences of my musical life was at a recital that Glenn played at Massey Hall in Toronto. He played a performance of Beethoven's Sonata in E Major, Opus 109 that moved me as few other pianists had ever done. I had played a lot of Beethoven when working with Guerrero, but never this sonata. I looked at it and decided that apart from a long series of trills in the last movement on which I would have to do a lot of work, I could handle the piece technically.

I had always loved Chopin, but I was never satisfied with what I was able to do with his repertoire. One time, after a depressing day of teaching in Hamilton, I noticed that the Polish pianist Witold Małcuzinsky was to give a recital that night. His reputation was that of a big technique basher, so I had never been particularly interested in hearing him play. He had a fascinating publicity picture that made him look like an axe-murderer. When he came out on the stage, I thought I was in the wrong spot. Out walked this tall, blond, god-like person who didn't in the least resemble his picture. His playing, far from being simply technical, was poetic and touching. He had just discovered Debussy and he played a big group of his pieces with terrific flair and delicacy. At the end of the program he played a short group of Chopin — a mazurka, a waltz, and an impromptu, none of them especially demanding from a technical standpoint, but how he played them! I thought immediately that here was what was missing in my Chopin playing — a sense of the soul of the music that perhaps you have to be Polish to truly understand. Of course, there have been many excellent Chopin players who weren't Polish — Guerrero, for instance, was a beautiful interpreter of Chopin, but Małcuzinsky brought something that I'd never heard before — a sense of lightness, elegance, and colour, which I suppose is the essence of this music. Although I knew that this Scottish-Irish kid from Regina was never going to turn into a Pole, I was inspired by this recital to include the 24 Preludes of Chopin for my New York program.

By general consensus, the second Book of Préludes by Debussy was the most successful thing I did on the Debussy series at the music library in 1962, so, in order not to burden myself with too much new repertoire, I programmed them for the second half of my projected recital.

Now, all I had to do was to learn and polish this repertoire and I'd be all set. Of course, it turned out to be a much bigger project than I had thought, but at least I was getting my way out of the stagnation of working in Hamilton.

When, in June of 1967, I was nearly ready to play my program for friends, I got a phone call from an actor, Don Cullen. He had acted on Broadway in the British satirical review *Beyond the Fringe*. He was involved in a revival of the show and he needed a pianist to do the Dudley Moore role. He got my name from an actress, Joyce Campion, who had worked with me on her voice. He told her that he was looking for a crazy pianist. She said, "I know a very crazy pianist," and Don came to interview me. He asked me to play something, so I played a couple of my flashiest numbers from the recital. He said, "We open in Buffalo in three weeks. Do you want to do it?" I asked him if he wanted to hear me read some of the lines. "No, I can tell that you're mad enough to be what we want."

I was immediately plunged into an entirely different world. I took my sister Patsy, already a highly respected actress in Toronto, to lunch and said, "Okay, Patsy. How does one do the acting thing?"

"Are you kidding," she yelled. "You think you can learn to act over lunch?"

"Cut the drama, honey. Just tell me what to do."

She gave me a few tips, but I could tell that she was exasperated. It was all a big laugh.

Speaking of which, when we got into rehearsal, the other three guys were so brilliantly funny that I could never get my lines out. I would try to deliver the words and would have to stop because I was laughing so hard. Of course, part of it was the terrific script, but also, I wasn't in any way prepared to deal with their skills. They were very good about it; they simply said, "We'll just wait for you to get yourself under control."

I finally got a hold of myself and we opened at the Studio Arena

Theatre. As we were standing in the wings waiting to go on, Barry Baldero, an incredibly funny and inventive actor, grabbed my arm and hissed, "Now Stuart, don't go up on your lines." I could have killed him. We went on. The show started with me playing the first few bars of "The Star Spangled Banner" and the other actor in the troop, Roy Wordsworth, had the line "Very good, Buffy, I think you've almost got it." Barry had the next line. "By the way, when are you going to America?" Roy delivered his line and we all looked at Barry.

Big Blank.

He smiled beatifically and crossed his legs. The dramatic tension couldn't be sustained by this insouciance, so I jumped in with a version of his line and then added my own line. As soon as I started speaking, he remembered his line and came out with something like "Ah. Yes. That's it, isn't it?" Smile.

After the show, I shrilled at him, "Barry, for god's sake, what was that?"

"Well." He smiled. "I like to keep my performance fresh."

"Fresh? That was our first performance." It was an indication of what was to come. Barry was infinitely funny, and he gave a different performance each night for the entire run.

The reviews in Buffalo were great and we played to sold out houses for the four-week run. We then came to Toronto and opened at the upstairs cabaret at Old Angelo's Restaurant. It was a huge success with the public, although, as usual in Toronto, the critics were less than enthusiastic. One critic said that my performance was a combination of Hildegard and Carol Channing. When I told a gay friend of mine in New York, he said, "Never mind, darling. Those are very big people."

In spite of the critics, we ran for six months in Toronto. It was enormous fun and I loved doing it. The only problem was that with eight shows a week there was no time to try out my New York recital program.

I asked Greta Kraus if she would listen to it and she eagerly agreed to do so. After I had played the Beethoven sonata, she was rather evasive, but she said that she was surprised at how good the fugal passage of the variations in the last movement sounded.

We went on to the Chopin. She said, "I know nothing about Chopin, but let's hear it anyway." When I had finished the preludes, she said, "Very good, excellent."

But then came the Debussy.

Greta was a real Viennese. Debussy and Vienna have never been a match, and if she confessed to not knowing about Chopin, Debussy was *terra incognita* for her.

When I finished, she said, "Oh, my dear, the Debussy was international first-class playing. You're so clever to put it at the end, because everyone will have forgotten about the Beethoven."

"Darling, I *have* to play the Beethoven."

"Yes, of course. It's all right, but the Debussy will wipe the Beethoven out of everyone's mind."

When the time came for the New York recital, I took the weekend off from the show. I played the two shows Friday night, went to New York, did the recital, and was back in the show on Tuesday.

The New York concert wasn't bad. I was horribly nervous, as I felt that I hadn't played the program in public enough to give me the kind of confidence I needed. I was very much afraid of the Chopin G-major Prelude No. 3. I could never get the left hand to go fast enough. It was the one number on the program that I felt I shouldn't be trying to play.

The night before the concert, some friends of mine who had come down to New York for the performance took me out for a glamorous dinner at Churchill's near the UN building. At the restaurant, there was a tiny African-American girl playing cocktail piano. Suddenly, in the midst of dinner, my hair stood straight up on my head. She was playing the G-major Prelude and she was playing it about five times faster than I could manage it. I shot across the room and told her that I was making my debut at Towne Hall the next afternoon and that I was playing that prelude.

I asked her if she could show me the fingering she used. She was very sweet and there, before the whole restaurant, she gave me a lesson on the prelude.

I spent most of the night trying to get the new fingering into my mind, and when I got to the hall — they gave you one hour to practise before the concert — I spent the whole time working on the prelude with its new fingering. I don't know what possessed me to do such a stupid thing, but I wasn't thinking very rationally at that moment.

When my practice time was up, a violinist arrived with his accompanist. The accompanist turned out to be the famous film composer Elmer

Bernstein. He introduced himself and said, "You're playing at five and we're playing at two. You should go to the office and check the marquee, because it says that at five o'clock there is a debut recital by Stuart Bernstein. Perhaps you should get that straightened around."

Five o'clock came. I shot out onto the stage with my right hand in the G-sharp B position so that I could at least get the Beethoven going. Before my bum even hit the piano bench I was playing G-sharp B. What happens in the sonata is that you play broken chords for eight bars and then the music slows down into a beautiful recitative section. I got to the recitative and suddenly I felt that I had been hit at the bottom of my back with a baseball bat. I kept going but then it happened again. I thought, *If it happens one more time, I'm going to have to lie down on the stage and cry.* Fortunately, it didn't happen again, but I was sweating so much that my glasses kept sliding off my nose. I spent almost as much time pushing them back up as I did playing the Beethoven. The pain, it turned out, was the nerves at the base of my spine, which had gone into a spasm.

I went into the Chopin. I played the first two preludes and then made a big fuss about adjusting the piano bench and looking around the hall. Then I skipped the third prelude and slid into the fourth. The next day in the *New York Times*, the reviewer said that I had played the 24 Preludes of Chopin with great sensitivity. I hadn't. I had played twenty-three of them. Martha came from Regina for the concert and said afterward, "I loved the Chopin." So, Abraham Lincoln was right. You can fool some of the people some of the time.

The review was very good, certainly not a rave, but very nice and respectful. I got a call from Columbia Artists Management. They had read the review and they asked me if I were planning another recital in New York. I was still recovering from this one. "If you do another one, let us know, and we'll send a representative to hear it." I put this into the back of my mind and went back to Toronto and to *Beyond the Fringe*.

The show played throughout the winter and then went on tour to Quebec, after which we did a big tour of the Maritimes, ending up at the Charlottetown Festival, where we performed for the summer.

In the meantime, I had determined to play another program in New York. I felt that I hadn't given myself enough preparation time for the first recital and I wanted to play the new program as much as possible before returning. I spoke to my brother Peter about lending me the money to do a series of performances across Canada in preparation for the second concert. I explained that, while I had no illusions about becoming a great piano virtuoso, I thought that in order to fulfill my commitment to a career in music, I had to push myself as far as I thought I could.

He generously agreed to lend me the considerable amount to cover the costs of recitals in Vancouver, Calgary, Regina, Winnipeg, Montreal, and Toronto, and then, of course, in New York. I hired a girl in Toronto who had done the publicity for *Beyond the Fringe* and she took care of all the bookings and travel arrangements.

She did what she could, but the audiences were small, to put it mildly. In Calgary, twelve people showed up and three of them were critics.

I had chosen a program much more suited to my talents and limitations: the Haydn F-minor Variations, a big group of Debussy, including six of the Études, and, after intermission, a group of Brahms intermezzi and Mussorgsky's "Pictures at an Exhibition." At the end of the Mussorgsky, you do everything except sit on the keyboard. With the tiny houses I attracted across the country, I would thunder through to the end, at which time there would be a *pat pat pat* from the audience before I skittered off the stage to dead silence.

In spite of the tiny houses, those concerts were an invaluable experience for me and, in spite of savage reviews in Toronto (a typical one said that I looked like a member of the Goon Squad. Not that one could necessarily argue about that, but it didn't tell you much about my abilities or lack of them, for playing the piano), I was much more confident going into the second concert in New York.

I had worked the program with Weldon Kilburn. He was a respected piano teacher in Toronto and an excellent accompanist for the great Canadian soprano Lois Marshall. He was a very erratic guy; many times I would show up for a lesson and he would have forgotten our appointment. But I admired his passion for music, and his suggestions, particularly about the Haydn and Debussy, were most helpful and revelatory.

After the debacle of the Toronto concert, Weldon phoned me and said, "How do you feel?"

"I feel like I've been run over by a truck."

"I want you to come and work through the program with me every day before you leave for New York." He was living with Lois Marshall at the time, so I went to their place and worked every day with him. Lois later told me that she was astonished to hear us going at one another: "I realized that there were two really big personalities there." Actually, Weldon and I had similar ideas; it was simply a question of coming to some sort of mutual understanding. In the end, the lessons were tremendously helpful in giving me something to hold onto after the devastating and insensitive Toronto reviews.

When I played my concert in New York six days later, I received an excellent and thoughtful review in the *New York Times*. The general tenor of the review was that, although my technique was not of virtuoso calibre, "virtuosos are a dime a dozen these days, whereas this sensitivity and musicality is in rare supply." It certainly was an improvement on the Toronto reviews.

For this second and, as far as I was concerned, last New York concert, I decided to put on the dog. I rented a suite at the Hotel Pierre and had a big party after the concert. While I was in Calgary I had bought one of my favourite fetish fashion outfits, a jeans suit made of cork-coloured leather. I bought a pair of cowboy boots to go with it and I thought I looked terrific. A week before my concert, Richard Nixon had been elected president of the United States and he was living at the Pierre. The management had replaced all the carpets in the lobby and they were very thick and impressive. However, I wasn't used to walking in my new cowboy boots and the pointy toes dug into the rugs and at one point I went down flat on my face, somewhat modifying the butch impression that I was attempting to achieve.

That evening, I went out to practise, but when the doors of the elevator opened there was a crowd of reporters with flash bulbs going off all over the place. I thought, *Wow! This agent has done a great job of publicizing my concert.* I then realized that the reporters were all facing in the other direction. Out of the opposite elevator stepped Nixon and his flunkies. I slunk off to my rehearsal.

Two hours before the concert, I received a phone call from the woman who was handling the arrangements. She said, "I haven't yet received the deposit for the hall."

"But I sent it to you in August." — This was November.

"I didn't get it, and they won't let us in to the hall until they get their money."

STUART HAMILTON
pianist

TUES. EVE., NOV. 26 • at TOWN HALL • 8:30 p.m.

Brochure for my second recital in New York City, 1968. One Toronto paper described me as looking like a member of the Goon Squad.

It was already five o'clock. They wanted the money by seven or the whole thing was off.

They wouldn't take a personal cheque on a Canadian bank unless it was certified. The banks were closed. Panicky, I phoned around to my friends in New York. There was a couple with whom I had worked at the theatre in Buffalo, Alan and Renee Leicht. Alan immediately said, "That's ridiculous that they're putting you through this just before you play. I don't have the money, but they'll take an American cheque, so I'll write one and you can arrange it with your Toronto bank in the morning." Alan gave them the cheque, for which there were no funds in his account, and the concert went on.

I played the recital, and the next morning called my bank in Toronto and ordered the money to be sent to Alan's account. Two months later, the agent phoned to say that she had just received the cheque that I had sent in August. What had happened was that there had been a mail strike in Canada and my money order had been caught up in the confusion.

After the concert, I had a big party at my suite at the Pierre. Going up in the elevator, a very distinguished gentleman got on and said, "You seem to be having a great time."

I said, "Yes, we are. I've just played a recital at Towne Hall and we're going to have a great party in my suite. Why don't you drop by?"

He replied, "I'd love to come, but I have a meeting to go to. If it's okay, I'll drop by later." I allowed that that would be fine and he introduced himself as Gore Vidal. He never did show up.

The bartender supplied by the hotel turned out to be Lady Bird Johnson's favourite one and so everything was very jolly. He loved Roxolana Roslak, a beautiful pupil of mine. He was Czech and she Ukrainian, so they understood each other and they taught us all how to drink vodka *à la Russe* and everyone was very happy.

Roxolana was on her way to Europe and she stayed with me that night at the hotel. When we went to bed, quite tanked, she said, "Don't you think you should get married, Stuart?"

"What?"

"There is a girl in Toronto who I know who is crazy about you."

"Roxolana, please. I've just played a recital in New York and I'm dead, exhausted, and drunk."

"Too bad," she murmured and we turned over and went to sleep.

The next day, I got another call from Columbia Artists. Their representative had found the concert interesting and they said that they would like to try me out as one of their artists on their Celebrity Concert Series. I was thrilled, as this was the goal of all the pianists of my generation.

They arranged for me to do three recitals in the Toronto area. But before it all came to pass, they called me to say that all three venues had cancelled their series for the next season. It was the beginning of the end of the Columbia Artists "farming program." I was, of course, sorry to miss the opportunity, but I had really accomplished what I wanted from my New York recital project. I was ready to get on with my life as an accompanist and vocal coach.

Chapter 7

New Adventures

I went back to Toronto, picked up my teaching again, and began to pay off the loan from Peter. I was making enough money, even though I had spent most of it on these two recitals. I also got an invitation to go back to Buffalo to conduct there. They were doing a big production of *HMS Pinafore*. Studio Arena Theatre was spending much more than usual on the show because it was to be broadcast live by ABC-TV. I agreed to conduct the orchestra. Of course, I had never conducted an orchestra in my life, but Gilbert and Sullivan is hardly the most demanding repertoire in the world.

There was a little tiny orchestra similar to those used at teatime in hotels — a palm court orchestra — with about five players. We started the first rehearsal and everything bounced along very well. At the end of the overture they sort of didn't finish, but just dribbled off. I beat four beats and that was the end, and I thought that was all I had to do.

"How do I get you guys to stop?" I asked.

They stared at one another. The cellist, a smartass kind of guy, said, "Well, you make the sign to stop."

"How do you do that?"

So the cat was out of the bag: they realized that I knew nothing about conducting. They told me how to do it and I did the cut-off sign, and they all stopped; it was a miracle. They thought it was pretty funny, but they could see that I knew what to do with the spirit of the music. Anybody can conduct Gilbert and Sullivan. It's so skillfully put together that all you have to do is have enthusiasm and the shows practically run themselves. The musicians were all very good and there was no problem. Near the end of the run, one of them told me that they were rather startled when they saw that I didn't know what I was doing. "But," he said, "you learned fast."

Opening night was a coast-to-coast, live television performance. The rehearsals had been great fun and everyone was looking forward to doing the show. Act 1 was terrific. We started the second half, and the first piece is "Fair Moon, To Thee I Sing," the baritone aria. The second, number fourteen in the score — I'll never forget it — is the duet between Buttercup and the Captain, "Things Are Seldom What They Seem." The introduction goes *chung, chung, CHUNG*. I conducted that, and half the orchestra played *chung, chung, CHUNG*. The other half played *Ladi, di, di* — the opening of number fifteen. I froze.

"Number fourteen," I hissed. I did it again and there was indescribable cacophony. This was live on national television; I was freaking. I finally realized what had happened. The concertmaster had forgotten that we were at fourteen rather than fifteen, so he was playing fifteen and the rest of us were trying to play number fourteen. I dived at the piano and banged out the introduction to number fourteen as hard as I could, and then gave the downbeat. The two people on stage were absolutely like statues of salt. They could not move; they could not make a sound.

I screamed at Buttercup, "Things are seldom!" and swung into action. That finally got them going, but that woman never spoke to me again for the rest of the run. I went to apologize but she wouldn't open her door. I tried to explain, but a conductor is not supposed to let that sort of thing happen. Well, this is what convinced me that I was not interested in conducting.

However, I did conduct eight more shows with the Studio Arena Theatre — A *Funny Thing Happened on the Way to the Forum*; *Stop the World, I Want to Get Off*; *Dames at Sea*, all sorts of Broadway shows. There's nothing to it. They hire people who are in the milieu and know how to do it. You rehearse them for three weeks. You play the rehearsals on the piano and so you get to know the shows by the time it comes to the orchestral rehearsal. The orchestra musicians in Buffalo were excellent. They were all Italians.

Patsy moved back to Toronto from the United States where she had been living and working with her husband, actor Les Carlson. She came to Toronto because she was pregnant and she wanted the baby to be born in Canada. While I was in Buffalo, she moved me out of my apartment and into a house with them. When she picked me up at the bus station, she said, "Oh, by the way, you're not living where you used to." She had moved into a big house, which would accommodate us all. Talk about a nesting instinct. It turned out to be a great place, and I lived there for almost fourteen years. It had six bedrooms and over the years it served as a temporary dorm for everyone in the family, plus a lot of passers-through. It has since been torn down.

Mother lived with us for about five years. She was always very agitated when we had guests. On one occasion, Alan and Renee Leicht visited from Buffalo. The morning after their arrival, I heard Mother banging around in the kitchen before dawn. I went downstairs to see what was going on and, as I stepped into the kitchen, she clutched at me like a harpy.

"Did you get the bangles?"

"What?"

"The bangles," she hissed. "Jewish people eat bangles and we don't have any."

"Mother, for heaven's sake, the word is *bagels*, and they don't *have* to have bagels." When the Leichts came down for breakfast, Mother ushered them into the dining room. It was a brilliant, hot, sunny summer morning, but Mother had pulled the drapes and the dining room looked like an inner sanctum from the Arabian Nights. The gloom was relieved by about three thousand glowing candles and every piece of crystal, china, and silver in the house was gleaming softly. Alan was dumbfounded, but Renee merely murmured, "How lovely," and proceeded to talk to mother about china patterns. Mother later allowed that the Leichts were a charming couple, but that it would have been much better if we had had bangles.

Patsy had the baby in August and he turned out to be Ben Carlson, who is now, forty years later, a great actor at the Shaw and Stratford Festivals. Two weeks later, they put the baby in the back of the Volkswagen and drove to Seattle to do an engagement there. I had fallen in love with this little baby. He was a week in the hospital and then he was home for a week.

He had his changing table in my bedroom and his favourite thing to do was to pee all over the wall while being changed. When they were about to leave, I had a great pang. Patsy said, "Well, you see, that's what you get for being gay. You finally get a baby and then they take it away from you."

During the last days of the run of Kurt Weill's *Lost in the Stars* in Buffalo, I received a call from a producer in New York City. He had been to see one of the performances and had been particularly impressed with my conducting (!) He was then producing *Mame* on Broadway and had just lost his music director. Could I come to New York City and step in? He mentioned the fee — for me it was beyond the dreams of avarice — and that I would have to be in New York within four days.

I said, "Oh, I'll have to get my work permit renewed."

"What work permit?"

"Well, I'm Canadian, so I have to have a work permit, and my current permit expires at the end of the Buffalo run. If you could call the immigration people, I'm sure that would arrange everything."

"Forget it. We haven't time."

"Well, let me try from my end. I'm sure it won't be a problem."

"Okay, but we have to know in two days." Click.

But it *was* a problem. I called everyone I could think of who might be able to help. I soon realized there was no way I could get even a temporary visa, let alone the notorious "green card," which would allow me to work in the States.

That night, I complained to the guys in the orchestra that a fortune — to say nothing of the musical opportunity — was slipping through my fingers. One of the men took me aside. "I might be able to help you. Let's have supper after the matinee tomorrow." My elation was short-lived. Another musician got me in a corner.

"What did that guy tell you?"

"He only said that he might help me get my work permit."

"Don't do it. His friends will get you the permit and then they'll own you."

"What are you talking about?"

"Believe me. Don't eat with him tomorrow. Eat with me — I mean it."

He was so urgent and sincere that I found an excuse to put off the first guy, who shrugged and said amiably, "No problem."

The next day, between shows, I met with musician number two. "Look at this," he said, pulling out a yellowing piece of newspaper with a picture of a weeping woman with two little boys. "That's me — on the left." The caption read: "Mob Implicated in Disappearance of Local Musician."

"My father tried to do a little rum-running on the side during Prohibition," he explained. "He was warned, but he ignored it. They gave him a cement overcoat and threw him over Niagara Falls. The guy who offered to help you is one of *them*."

The next day, I phoned the producers in New York City and told them I wasn't able to get the permit. I glumly returned to Toronto and put in my application for a green card through the regular channels. Eighteen months later, after numerous visits to the RCMP for mug shots, finger-printing, health certificates, residence affidavits (there was some interest in the fact that most of the buildings I had lived in had been torn down), and generally being made to feel like a crook, I got a notice that I was to appear at the U.S. Consulate-General in two weeks, with a stern warning that failure to appear with a chest X-ray from a designated doctor would result in another eighteen-month delay.

The day arrived and I presented myself at the doctor's office at seven in the morning. It was jammed with people. There was no sign of a doctor, but a couple of guys were snapping chests like mad, developing the X-rays, and collecting twenty bucks — cash only — from everybody. It was December. I trudged up University Avenue clutching my X-rays and was at the consulate at 8:15 a.m. An official at the door took the X-rays and directed me, "In there." "There" turned out to be a bare concrete room with row upon row of wooden benches and nothing else. It looked like a minimalist set for Menotti's opera *The Consul*. I took my place and waited.

Nothing.

At 10:00 we were startled by a booming voice over the loudspeaker: "Good morning. When your name is called, present yourself at Door B." We all shuffled with anticipation.

Nothing.

Eventually, The Voice boomed, "Doctor so and so." A man quickly got up and skittered through Door B.

Nothing.

The Voice: "Mrs. so and so." Same scene.

Nothing.

This process went on until about one o'clock in the afternoon. The rest of us looked haggard and desperate.

Nothing — for a really long time.

At 1:30 p.m., I said to one of the guards, "Is there somewhere one can buy something to eat?"

"No."

"I'm starving. I'm going out to get something."

"Go ahead, but if your name is called while you're not here, it's eighteen months before you'll get another appointment." I slunk back to my place, stomach roaring.

At 4:45 The Voice boomed, "Stuart Hamilton." I wobbled through Door B and into a small office where a large man was seated behind a desk. His uniform shirt had an enormous amount of badges on it. He shuffled through my papers and yelled, "Are you a homosexual?" For one giddy moment, I thought he was going to ask me for a date. I collected myself and thought, *This is no time for perjuring yourself or making a smartass remark.* So I answered, "I am not a *practising* homosexual." This statement was, strictly speaking, true. I was certainly not practicing right then. He grunted, pushing a paper at me. "Sign this. It's routine."

It was a document saying that, if recruited, I would go to fight in Vietnam. This was 1970, and the war in Southeast Asia was raging. I thought, *They're not going to take a forty-one-year-old*, so I signed.

Back to my bench.

By 6:15 I was beginning to hallucinate from hunger and exhaustion. It was then that a pretty, young woman came up to me and murmured, "Mr. Hamilton, the Consul would like a word with you."

Dazed, I followed her down a long corridor, through an outer office, and into an opulently furnished sitting room, brilliant with Stars and Stripes. Facing me, a huge, benevolently smiling photo of Richard Nixon was hanging on the wall.

I was introduced to the Consul, a strikingly handsome woman, and asked to take a seat. "I understand we are going to have you as a guest in our country," she said in a thrillingly modulated voice.

I wearily replied, "I hope so, Madam."

"I'm sorry it's taken so long, but you know how these governmental forms are. Ha, ha ha!"

Heh, heh, heh.

"Tell me," she said. "Have you lived in Toronto long?"

"A little over twenty years."

"Do you like it?"

"Yes, very much."

"Then why do you want to leave?"

Heads up!

"I've been offered several jobs in the U.S. and I've always felt one should be able, as a musician, to work wherever people feel you have the ability to do the job they have to offer."

I had the distinct impression that Madam was not interested in being lectured on the rights of artists. "My husband and I have just moved here from Vienna and we really regret that there is no chamber music available in Toronto."

Vibrating antennae.

I listed several venues in Toronto where one could hear excellent chamber music. "Well, I think that's all," she said, standing up.

I stood.

"Oh, by the way … (*watch it*) … can you tell me what this is?" She handed me a scrap of paper with the words *ondes Martenot* written on it.

About two years previously, I had been walking down Yonge Street in Toronto and I had stopped in front of a store that sold television sets. Ordinarily, nothing would induce me to watch television in those days, but I was intrigued to notice Leonard Bernstein on the screen. I went into the store and listened to him for several minutes. He was talking about the French composer Olivier Messiaen's fondness for an instrument that produced a wavy electronic sound — an *ondes Martenot*. If I hadn't been walking down that street and passed that store at that particular moment, I would never have had the slightest inkling what an *ondes Martenot* was.

Back to the Consulate General.

By now, I realized that our chatty little meeting was actually a *viva voce* upon which everything depended. I decided to be bold. "Madam," I said oilily, "do you speak French?"

Taken aback, she said, "Well, a little."

"Ah. Then you realize that the first word on your scrap of paper means 'waves.' This is the name of a musical instrument that produces a wavy sound, and it was invented by a man named Maurice Martenot. The composer Olivier Messiaen used it a lot."

"Welcome to the United States of America," she responded warmly.

The irony in all this is that I never got to use my precious green card and all the formality and frustrations went for nothing. One of the conditions of receiving the card was that within a week, one would establish residence in the United States. I duly went to New York City, where I stayed with friends and went to register for the draft. When I arrived at the local draft board, the guy at the reception desk looked at me in my leather drag and said, "Yeah, right."

Nevertheless, I registered and, of course, never heard from them. After a couple of days in New York, I got a call from Maureen Forrester, who asked me when I was coming back. She had lots of work to do and wanted to have me in Toronto. This was certainly *force majeure* for me. I happily gave up whatever opportunities might be waiting for me in the United States. With one of the great artists of our time waiting to work with me at home, I returned to Toronto immediately, became extremely busy, and have remained working in Canada ever since.

After my second recital in New York, I decided that I had accomplished what I set out to do: namely, that I had, through intensive practising, developed a respectable technique. I had also proved, to my own satisfaction, that I did not have the interest or talent to pursue a career as a solo pianist. The fallout from these two New York recitals, though not immediate, was considerable. Toronto music circles began to realize that I was something more than a clown and business picked up noticeably. There was no question of having to return to Hamilton to make a living.

In July 1970, the co-pilot of the Air Canada plane that my brother Peter, as pilot, was flying from Montreal to Toronto made a fatal error that resulted in the crash of the aircraft and the death of more than a hundred people on board, including my brother.

Peter's widow immediately told me she didn't want me to repay the rest of the loan. I felt that the money had been lent to me to further my career and that I had an obligation to spend it on another recital. I rejected the idea of another New York concert in spite of urging from Columbia Artists. I had decided that I wasn't capable of having a career as a solo pianist, so I determined to do something that I would enjoy. I settled on a program consisting of the two books of Debussy Préludes.

I took my first trip to Europe when I was forty-two years old. I felt that I had to experience some of the milieu that had formed the music to which I was devoting my life.

I went with my late friend Jacqueline White, whom I had met through Joy Alexander. Jackie was one of those beautiful women who gave off an emanation. When she walked into a room, every man responded. It's not that she was a vamp or that she did anything overt, but men seemed to get a message from her. She had friends to visit in Vienna. At that time, Vienna didn't interest me. Opera was my life, and I wanted to go to the birthplace of opera. We arranged to meet in Venice. When we got together, she told me of her arrival in Venice. She was completely confused at the station, but — true to form — there was soon a man to help her. A porter arranged for her to get some Italian currency, fetched her luggage, arranged for transportation to her hotel, and bought her a cup of coffee. "But when I tipped him, he looked at me in the strangest way," she said.

"How much did you give him?"

"The largest coin I had." She showed me.

"But, darling, this is worth four cents." When we were leaving Venice, we ran into this same porter and showered him with thousands of lire.

The trip was fabulous: Venice, Florence, Nice, Paris, and London. Glorious music everywhere.

I loved everything we did and saw; so when I had the opportunity for one last solo concert, it had to be in Europe. Carrol Anne Curry was one of the singers who worked with me at that time. I had met her when she was Susanna to Libby's Countess in *The Marriage of Figaro*. She had recently had a great coup in getting the role of Despina in the Scottish National Opera's production of Mozart's *Così fan tutte*. The rest of the cast was very starry indeed: Janet Baker, Elizabeth Harwood, and John Shirley-Quirk. Carrol Anne had a success and was planning a Wigmore recital debut in London. She encouraged me to come to London for her concert and to do mine the following week. And so I made my "Farewell Debut."

Backstage at Wigmore Hall, there is a large mirror in the wings, I suppose so you can check to see if your fly's done up before going on. I looked at myself and thought, *Why are you doing this agonizing thing to yourself? And what's more, it's costing you a fortune.*

I didn't play very well in London; I misjudged the acoustics of the hall. Carrol Anne came back at intermission and said, "Stop murmuring up there. We can't hear you." I had thought that with the bright sound of the hall, I was playing too loudly. The reviews were respectful, but I knew that my performance was only adequate. While I felt that I had fulfilled my obligations to Peter's loan and memory, I was glad that my solo piano career was at an end.

Chapter 8

Many Stars

When I returned from London, I had a wonderful surprise in store. Lois Marshall asked me to play a series of concerts with her. I had known Lois ever since our meeting in 1948 at Gerald Moore's classes. I had followed her brilliant career from her appearance in Beethoven's *Missa Solemnis* with Toscanini to her unprecedented six tours of the Soviet Union, where she was worshipped. I was terribly elated about playing for her and I eagerly anticipated our rehearsing together. However, Lois had a vast repertoire and had sung it all over the world, so she was not interested in rehearsing it again: we had one rehearsal. I kept saying, "What's your tempo for this song, darling?" She would reply, "Just play it, and we'll find the tempo."

Of course, she was right, and everything went beautifully. The first song on her program was Purcell's "Nymphs and Shepherds," an enchanting, deceptively simple piece. I played the introduction and Lois began. I immediately realized that I was in a totally different performance mode than I had ever experienced before. I had to pull up my socks to keep up with her. Fortunately, all went well, and Lois was pleased, so we continued collaborating. I played nearly fifty concerts for her over the next decade, and every concert was a revelation.

I got to know Maureen Forrester through Mary Simmons, who was a great friend of Maureen's. Maureen had been living in Philadelphia and doing a bit of teaching. She moved to Toronto with her husband and children, and she needed a *repetiteur* (someone who helps you learn the notes) to work with her because she was preparing her debut role at the New York City Opera in Handel's *Julius Caesar*. This was the famous production in which Beverley Sills made her big breakthrough to stardom.

Maureen sang Cornelia, the leading contralto part. She came to work with me and we hit it off perfectly.

In the spring of 1975, I played a tour for Lois and Maureen in which they did duets and solos. We played in the Maritimes and in New England. To say that these two ladies were high-powered would be a ridiculous understatement. Backstage they were like two tanks ready to go and blast the audience out of their seats. I realized that one of my problems with performing had been that I was always trying to be calm before going on, whereas I saw that these two magnificent artists used their nerves to rev themselves up to give all they had. And their "all" was astonishing. Nonetheless, they were quite different personalities: Lois was as profoundly spiritual (in the artistic sense) as anyone I've ever come across. When she was on, which was most of the time, she was perfectly aware of the message she was conveying and its effect on her listeners. Maureen was all instinct. It didn't matter which composer or style, Maureen was able to get to the heart of a song and deliver its essence with maximum impact. Maureen loved her audiences, but I saw her many times when she seemed to be surprised at the effect her performances had on the public. Both ladies were far too classy to be rivals, but there was a certain competitive edge to their work together: they spurred each other on. Their duets were models of ensemble and artistic excitement. Playing for them was one of the highlights of my musical life.

It was also exhausting. The day of a concert, Lois was totally incognito. She wouldn't even answer her phone. About four o'clock in the afternoon, we would realize she was still alive, because she would begin to vocalize. She had a light snack about five, and the vocalizing would continue until it was time to leave for the concert. In contrast, Maureen would spend the day exploring the city, shopping for antiques, or having her hair done. We would eat a regular supper, pick up Lois, and head off.

After the show, Lois had all this energy she had been storing up all day. She would want to eat and have a party. Maureen and I would go to her room and Lois would order room service. Maureen would have a snack, a couple of drinks, and then go off to bed. However, Lois was just starting. She had a great sense of humour and an inexhaustible supply of riotous stories, so it was always great fun. Nonetheless, it did certainly go on: often until two or three in the morning. I would stagger off to my room and collapse in a heap only to have Maureen banging at my door at 7:30 or 8:00 the next morning. "Come on, Stuart. I saw a terrific store I want to explore. Get up."

His Master's Voice. When I got back from that tour, I had black circles around my eyes that wouldn't have looked out of place on a raccoon.

I mentioned much earlier in this narrative about the dangers of a coach being too involved with his/her pupils. This trait dies hard, and the last two people for whom I tried to do everything were Carrol Anne Curry and Roxolana Roslak. We've already briefly met them.

When I first met Roxolana, she was celebrated for her beautiful voice and her numerous boyfriends. Both these women were very talented, but in quite different ways. Carrol Anne was really a *diseuse*. I have rarely come across any soprano who could get the text across to an audience the way she could. She was good at languages, but the extraordinary thing was her enunciation in English. English is a notoriously difficult language to sing, especially for high voices. There was little love lost between Carrol Anne and Roxolana, but one time I took Roxy to hear Carrol Anne sing in a performance of Berlioz's *The Damnation of Faust*, being performed in English, and Roxy (who always has had a great sense of fairness — on top of which, her own diction left something to be desired) said at the end, "I could understand every word that woman sang."

Roxy, on the other hand, was mainly sound. She is of Ukrainian descent and she had the soft, ravishing quality that often distinguishes the singing of the southern Slavic people. As well, she had an innate sense of music combined with an absolutely fearless commitment. I passionately believed in these women and although their careers were progressing, it was at a snail's pace. When Roxy's finances finally required her to take a job selling handbags at Birk's, a jewellery store, I felt something had to be done.

In the fall of 1973, the owner of the Italian restaurant The Dell phoned and asked me if I could get Maureen Forrester to do a show for the Cabaret Theatre he had above his restaurant. Naturally, Maureen was far too busy to commit herself to a long run in a cabaret — or anywhere else for that matter — but I came up with the idea of doing a mini-opera, a short version of Puccini's *La Bohème*. The owner was all for it and asked me to develop a budget. With the help of John Leberg, who was working as Geiger-Torel's assistant at the COC, I put together something that wouldn't cost too much, and we were in business.

Roxy sang Mimi, Rudolfo was Roelof Oostwoud, John directed, and I played the little upright piano. We started with the magical entrance of Mimi because we only had a cast of five instead of the original ten-plus chorus. In order to get the performances started, we needed some sort of introduction. It was decided that I would sit at the piano and play some of Musetta's waltz. There would be a phone on the piano, and when it rang I would pick it up and say, "Hello, Bohème? You're going to your first performance of *La Bohème?* Oh, you'll love it." I would then launch into a synopsis of the story, and describe the setting and background. Eventually, I would get to Mimi's entrance and off we went.

The opening was greeted rather coolly by the critics, but then, by good fortune, the owner of the *Toronto Star*, the biggest paper in town, came to a performance early on and adored it. The next weekend there was a full-page story on the front page of the Entertainment section, and we were all set. *Hello, Bohème*, as we called it, ran for nearly a hundred performances.

Looking back, I don't know how we did it: seven shows a week with two shows on Friday and Saturday evenings. And in those days everyone smoked. By the second show on Saturday, you could hardly see the stage for smoke. The baritone, Avo Kittask, and I did every performance. After a couple of weeks, Roelof got a contract in Europe and he was replaced by Michael Burgess, who had vocal chords of steel and sang every performance for the rest of the run. (The rest of the cast had understudies who sang some of the shows.) The restaurant's owner was delighted and we immediately began planning another show for the fall based on Puccini's *Tosca*. However, finances fell through and it never happened.

In the early winter of the 1973–74 season, Columbia Artists phoned Lois and asked her to recommend an accompanist for a tenor who was to give the first solo recital at the newly inaugurated arts centre in Hamilton. Lois suggested me for the job, I spoke to the lady at Columbia, and all was arranged. As the conversation drew to a close, I said, "May I ask the name of the tenor?"

"Oh, yes. José Carreras."

Carreras was near the beginning of his career at that point, but he had already made a big stir at the New York City Opera. When he came to my very modest house on Pleasant Boulevard, he looked like ten million dollars in a full-length black mink coat. He was charming and down-to-earth and the rehearsal was fine until we got to a group of songs by Bellini. Like most Bellini, these songs have beautiful melodies with simple accompaniments. I began the first song. "Oh, Mr. Hamilton, I'm so sorry, but I sing these songs up a fourth."

Not today, José.

I explained that I didn't transpose at sight, but that I would write out the transpositions and have them ready for the concert the next night.

"Wonderful."

We finished our rehearsal and arranged that I and my friends Joy Alexander and Peg McKelvey would pick him up the next day at his hotel. When he left, Patsy came out of the kitchen where she had been lurking and exclaimed, "Who in the name of heaven was that?" It was certainly true that voices like his were not heard every day in my studio.

I settled down to do the transpositions. Fortunately Bellini doesn't give the pianist much to do, so the task wasn't that onerous.

The next day, we picked Carreras up and drove him the forty miles to Hamilton. The hall was packed with a large contingent of Spanish people, there to support their fellow countryman. During the concert, I had a totally new experience. Carreras did a group of songs by Gabriel Fauré, beginning with the ecstatic "Après un Rêve." The song begins with six D-minor chords. As soon as I began, alarm bells went off in my head. Carreras hadn't taken a breath for the first phrase. I thought, *Oh my God, I've started the wrong piece*. I glanced at the program — *Après un Rêve*. I looked at him. He was looking at me with a lovely smile on his face. At this point I was on about chord number fourteen. I thought, *Why isn't he singing?*

I had a flashback. Several years before, I had turned pages for the accompanist of the great Swedish tenor Nicolai Gedda. I had been astonished to hear the accompanist give him a cue for most of the texts. What I didn't know was that in those days, singers who sang mostly opera were used to having a prompter. I had never been asked to do this, but it was obviously time to learn.

"Dans," I croaked.

Carreras smiled, turned to the audience, and sailed off into the song "Dans un sommeil." At that time, Carreras had one of the most beautiful voices I had ever heard. However, he was not immune to something that happens to everyone occasionally. He got stuck on one phrase of the text of a Spanish song and couldn't remember the next one. The phrase was *hasta la vista*. The song is by Manuel de Falla and the accompaniment is rather busy, so it was a while before I noticed that Carreras had sung *hasta la vista* at least ten times. I tried to give him the next line, but he couldn't hear me. Now, you can only say "I'll see you soon" so many times before it starts to sound odd. Finally he broke out laughing and came to look at the music. I told him what to say to the audience, which was holding its collective breath. "Ladies and Gentlemen," he declaimed in his rich Catalan accent, "Excuse me, but my Spanish is not so good."

With his youthful good looks, his magnificent voice, and his megawatt personality, he could do no wrong. The audience ate him up.

Chapter 9

Opera in Concert

In 1973, the Australian conductor Richard Bonynge was setting up a young artists program for the Vancouver Opera. He held auditions in Toronto and I played for a number of singers. One of them sang Ophelia's Mad Scene from Thomas' *Hamlet*. She had a score for the opera and I asked her to lend it to me so I could practise the accompaniment. One evening after supper I sat down and began reading through the score. Almost immediately I was struck by the quality of the music. *Hamlet* had been fairly popular from its first performance in 1868 until after the First World War, when it had slipped into almost total oblivion. I had played Ophelia's Mad Scene and Hamlet's Drinking Song, but I had never heard the whole opera. I finished playing the score about midnight and right away began planning how I could get this wonderful opera performed. At first I thought of performing it for a small audience at my studio.

However, I quickly realized that the work involved in preparing such a long, difficult piece demanded a larger platform.

Thus, the idea of Opera in Concert was born.

There were tons of operas, like *Hamlet*, which were languishing neglected on library shelves. Why not present a series of operas in concert, with piano accompaniment, no sets or costumes? It could be done economically and it would be an ideal platform for young artists to gain experience without the strain of having to carry an expensive production. The brain began to whirl. Why not rent a small concert hall, schedule three operas over a winter season, and see what happened? I had five thousand dollars in the bank, so I thought, *What the hell. I can do this. Andiamo!* My first season would be *Hamlet*, Berlioz's *Béatrice et Bénédict*, and Massenet's *Thaïs* — three wonderful operas, all with a past but no present. Until Opera in Concert.

Of course, there were many objections raised. Who would want to go to see an opera with no sets, costumes, acting, orchestra, or chorus? I have always believed that the music in opera is of a quality that can stand by itself, so I was undeterred.

In the world of opera, the person who has the most fun is the individual who does the casting. Imagining what voice will fit which role, and especially seeing that role come to life with the artist for whom you have chosen it is a tremendously satisfying experience. Roxy and her plight were the initial motivators behind Opera in Concert, but once it got going I was made aware — as never before — of the enormous pool of talent available in Canada. Opera in Concert's constitution states that its raison d'être is to present works outside the standard repertoire, with artists chosen from the Toronto area. Fulfilling this mandate has never been a problem.

Among singers from my own studio, Elizabeth Benson Guy had retired — much too early in my opinion — and Mary Simmons was to retire shortly after we began. However, there were many younger artists anxious to display their talents. Five thousand dollars, even in 1974, didn't go far in the music world, so I had to convince the nearly twenty singers needed for the first season to donate their services. As my actor-sister Pat has often said, "The arts in Canada are subsidized by the artists." Of course, everyone chipped in, I worked for nothing, and we got it off the ground.

Once we began rehearsals, I realized that there was far too much to do and that I would need an assistant. Carrol Anne had a friend, Kathryn Brown, who said she would work for peanuts, which is about what she got. She was a terrific friend, always cheerful and never discouraged, even in the thinnest days. She stayed with me, an invaluable help, for sixteen seasons.

In that first season, Carrol Anne had a triumph as Gertrude in *Hamlet*, Mary Simmons sang Béatrice in the Berlioz opera, and Roxy was a seductive Thaïs. Everything went well, but there was a big drama on opening night. The part of Hamlet in Thomas's opera is given, rather unusually, to a baritone — tenors are the norm for title roles. I had cast a tremendously gifted young man whom I thought would be perfect. As rehearsals progressed, I could see that, for whatever reason, my Hamlet was even more melancholy than the Dane he was portraying. This artist had a history of last-minute cancellations. I could see the whole project going down the drain — together with my five thousand dollars — before my eyes.

I hastily assembled a cast of understudies and began rehearsing them, just in case. The young man I had chosen to understudy the title role was newly arrived from Puerto Rico and he bore the resounding name of Guillermo (Bill) Silva-Marin. As the performance date approached, I said to Bill, "I don't think you're taking this seriously enough. If the other guy cancels and you have to go on and you don't know the role, I'll have you killed. It only costs seventy-five dollars to get someone killed in Toronto (this was in 1974; it's probably more now) and that's about all I'll have left when this is over — so you better buckle down — or else." Poor Bill's eyes got as big as saucers. I think he actually believed me.

At any rate, the inevitable happened. The morning of the show, I phoned the box office and, in my most unctuous tone, said, "This is Stuart Hamilton, the producer of Opera in Concert. Can you give me the number of seats sold for tonight's performance?"

"Sure," said the box office attendant. There was a short pause. "Three." As the telephone dropped to the floor through my lifeless fingers, I swore I would never again ask the attendance figures before a show (and I never have). However, worse was to come. The baritone's wife called to say that he was suffering from severe laryngitis (yeah, yeah, yeah) and wouldn't be able to sing. I called Bill and gave him the news that he was singing Hamlet that night, and the receiver dropped through *his* lifeless fingers.

In the event, there were about 150 people in the audience and Bill was a great success. He went on to have a twenty-five-year career, which took him to the Canadian Opera Company, the New York City Opera, and the Metropolitan Opera. He is now a successful stage director and, incidentally, since 1994, my successor as producer at Opera in Concert.

Our Ophélie that opening night was a zippy girl named Riki Turofsky who did a bang-up job of the Mad Scene. Riki has been an invaluable member of the Board of the Canada Council for the Arts and she is also one of the best fundraisers in Canada these days.

She and I have remained good pals and, twenty-eight years after *Hamlet*, I was having supper at her place (she is a terrific hostess) when during the conversation we discovered that her husband, Charles, had until recently owned Sterling Trust. (They actually had a huge French poodle named Sterling in memory of the company.) This, of course, was the company that my father had worked for in its Regina branch from 1928 to 1946, and Charles's grandfather, Charles Bauckham, had been Dad's boss.

Carrol Anne Curry and Guillermo Silva-Marin in Opera in Concert's *Hamlet*, 1977. *Photo by Robert C. Ragsdale.*

I vividly remember the annual visits of Mr. Bauckham (Dad called him "the Big Man from Toronto"). We always did our lower-middle-class best to put on the dog for these occasions, but something would invariably go wrong. One time a spare galosh was discovered at supper under the dining room table, and then there was the time I was delegated to entertain the BMFT while frantic preparations were going on in the kitchen.

At that time, about 1942, Dorothy had had a great success singing "Adieu Forêts" from Tchaikovsky's *The Maid of Orleans*. I knew nothing about the opera but I transfixed Mr. Bauckham for about half an hour with a completely fabricated story about Joan of Arc and Tchaikovsky's interpretation of her life. Fortunately the opera is rarely performed, so Mr. Bauckham was none the wiser. He was also very impressed. He later predicted to my father that I would someday be a commentator for the CBC.

Read on!

The Opera in Concert series was received rather coolly in the newspapers. The reviewers (in my opinion, Toronto has never had a real music critic) complained about what was not there — sets, costumes, chorus, orchestra — rather than what was. Fortunately for us, as has happened many times in Toronto, the public ignored the press. We sold more tickets than we had budgeted for and I gleefully set about planning our second season.

Kathy Brown was smart enough to insist that I acquire nonprofit status so that we could accept donations and give tax receipts. After the first season, we received a note from a Catholic priest with a donation of $2.50. I found this very touching, as I was fairly sure that this Divine had taken the vow of poverty and, thus, his little donation probably involved some considerable manipulation on his part. I wrote him a thank-you note and forgot about it.

The next season came another letter from the same man. You can imagine my astonishment when I opened it and found a check for fifteen thousand dollars. The priest turned out to be Father Edward Jackman, and indeed he had no money of his own, but as I understand it he has voting rights on the disbursement board of the Jackman Foundation and for the last thirty-five years he has consistently supported OIC with extraordinary generosity. Almost certainly, without his help Opera in

Concert would not be where it is today — one of the country's most efficacious platforms for young Canadian singers and a consistent source of pleasure and enlightenment for the opera lovers of Toronto.

Maureen told me that she had been to one of the OIC performances, that she thought the idea was terrific, and that she would like to sing one of the shows in the next season. Naturally, I was thrilled, but I told her we couldn't possibly afford her fee. "Nonsense," she retorted, "I don't want a fee. I think it's a wonderful thing for the kids, and I'd like to help get it going. Just find me a part and I'll let you know when I'm available." It took me about a minute and a half to make a choice. Our first two seasons were all French operas.

French opera in the latter half of the twentieth century was definitely the poor sister of the repertoire. Maureen was particularly famous for her Mahler, but she was a native of Montreal, she spoke French, and I knew, with her creamy sound and exquisite phrasing that she would be perfect for Charlotte in Massenet's *Werther*. She loved the idea and said, "Just find me a wonderful tenor, and I'll do it."

I learned that there was a young man with an impressive voice at the opera school at the University of Toronto. His name was Paul Frey. I called him and invited him to come and sing for me. He was excited when I explained the project to him and I asked him to learn some of the score — the aria "Pourquoi me réveiller" and the first-act "Clair de Lune" scene. In a couple of weeks he came back with them memorized and sung them beautifully, so I had Maureen come to hear him. She was thrilled and so all was arranged.

We opened our second season with an interesting double bill. After her big hit in *Hamlet*, I wanted something special for Carrol Anne. She had done a couple of performances in concert of Poulenc's monodrama *La Voix humaine* and I thought it would be great for Opera in Concert, but with a simple staging. The problem was to find something to go with it, as it takes under an hour to perform. I got the idea to precede it with a performance in an English translation of the play by Jean Cocteau on which Poulenc based his opera. And who better as the actress than my sister Patsy. I felt it sort of made up for all the threats that I used to make in Regina to drown her in the cistern. Both girls were great and the show caused a certain buzz in Toronto's musical world.

But the big excitement was about Maureen's singing in *Werther* — and who was this tenor who was singing his first leading role opposite Mighty Maureen? As it happened, Maureen was singing Ulrica in Verdi's *Un Ballo in Maschera* at the Metropolitan in New York at the same time as we were having our final rehearsals. As always, she had worked out her schedule so that she could fulfill her commitments in both cities. However, nothing works exactly the way it should. The Met had some unexpected changes in cast and they needed Maureen for unscheduled rehearsals. I was on the verge of panic, but Maureen was totally in control. "I'll just fly down to New York in the mornings and be back here for rehearsals in the evenings. No problem."

It was early December, with very uncertain weather conditions for flying. This made for a tense week of rehearsals, but nothing fazed Maureen. She flew back and forth to New York four times that week and she was in terrific voice at all times. Paul was naturally very nervous, but we had worked hard and he was ready. He had made it clear that he would not take the final bow at the end of the opera, because he felt that, even though he was singing the title role, the public was there because of Maureen. I just wanted to get through the damned opera by this point, so I agreed. However, we reckoned without Madame.

The stage manager was my nephew Doug Marshall, Dorothy's son. Doug is a big bear of a man and Paul is very slender, so Maureen had arranged for Doug to put his arms around Paul at the bows, and she dashed out to take her bow first. Paul was furious, but Maureen was already receiving her ovation and there was nothing to be done. When Paul finally took his bow, there was a huge roar from the audience and Maureen turned to me, "You see, I was right. The opera *is* called *Werther*, after all."

The next day Maureen and I flew down to New York and I saw her performance that night at the Met, after which we went out and had a champagne supper at Sardi's to celebrate.

The next season, Lois and Maureen were engaged to do a concert at Toronto's venerable Massey Hall. I was very excited about doing this performance, as I had never played a full recital in this ramshackle hall with its beautiful acoustics.

The week of the concert, Massey Hall was fully booked, so we didn't get a stage rehearsal. This didn't matter to the girls, as they had both sung there countless times, and the program was basically the same as they had done the year before on tour. However, I was anxious to try the piano and get an idea of the acoustics from the stage, so I managed to get an hour and a half at six o'clock that evening after a symphony rehearsal.

When I got to the hall, the superintendent said that he was going on his supper break so he would lock me in and be back in an hour.

I sat at the piano and started the first song of the Brahms' *Zigeunerlieder*, which Maureen was singing that night as her solo group. My hair nearly fell out from shock. The piano was ghastly. The top sounded like broken glass and the bottom notes were like atomic bombs going off. I would have to practise for a month before I would be able to play this stupid instrument. What was I going to do? I frantically looked over the vast stage and my eyes fell on another piano that had been pushed over to the corner.

Luckily it was unlocked. I ran my fingers over the keys and was transported. Then I remembered that a big star pianist was playing with the orchestra that week and this was probably his instrument. I was alone in the huge building. The pianos looked exactly alike but the quality of the two instruments was like night and day. This was an important concert for me. If I just switched instruments …

If I were discovered, all they could do to me was switch them back, right?

Hee! Hee! Hee!

I spent the whole hour shoving these enormous instruments around that stage, and when the caretaker came back from supper I was innocently practising on the great piano, while the rotten one lurked in the shadows.

"Everything okay?" he asked.

"Fine," I quavered.

Imagine my relief when I walked on stage to do the concert to find that my subterfuge had gone undetected and I got to do the concert on this gorgeous instrument. Crime sometimes *does* pay.

Everything went beautifully; the girls were magnificent and the audience was *en délire*, as the French say.

The only hitch happened right at the end. The ladies had run through their repertoire of encores, but the audience was vociferously demanding more.

Lois said, "Oh, let's do the Bach."

I stiffened. "What Bach?"

"You know, 'Wir Eilen,' the famous duet."

"I've heard you guys do it, but I've never played it," I shrilled.

"You can read it. It's not hard."

"But what's the tempo?"

Maureen: "Da-da-ta-da-da."

Lois; "No, no, no, that's too fast. It's DA-DA-ta-DA."

The door to the stage opened and we went on — me with death in my heart. It became heartattacksville when I opened the music. It was figured bass. That is, all that's printed is the bass line and a lot of numbers, 5/3, 6/4, 7/5, to indicate the harmony. This is not an insurmountable problem for a musician who has been properly trained, but that didn't include me.

Maureen announced the duet and there were more cheers from the audience. There was nothing to be done. I plunged in. I played the bass line with all the baroque energy I could muster and feathered in some sort of harmony — mostly wrong. Once again, the girls were magnificent.

However, Bach is not known for concision and the damned piece went on and on while I sweated like a pig. I heaved a sigh of relief when I turned the last page and then froze. At the bottom of the page were the fatal words *da capo*, meaning "go back to the beginning."

The whole thing was a blur, but somehow we finished and the audience exploded again. While the ladies were taking their bows, I hid the rest of the music in the men's room — just in case they decided to spring another number on me.

After the concert, there was great animation backstage. I saw Greta heading for me and I groaned. "Oh God, here comes 'L'Esprit de Bach.'"

"Stuart," she cried, "You played really well."

"Even the Bach, Greta?"

"Even the Bach. Actually, you played so well, I couldn't believe it was you."

Many years later I was at a party given by my friends Eric Hood and his wife, Clarissa Barton. Eric said, "Sit down, Stuart. I want you to listen to something." With that, he put on a tape that turned out to be of Lois and Maureen singing the Bach duet at that concert in Massey Hall. He had been there and snuck in a tape recorder. I listened with grisly fascination to my attempts at realizing the figured bass, and to my astonishment it wasn't at all bad. It's amazing what adrenaline will do.

As an accompanist, encores were my bugaboo. Nobody wants to practise encores. You are constantly being told, "Oh, I'll probably just sing so-and-so. It's not hard. You can sight-read it," or "We won't need any more encores. Forget it."

Yeah, yeah, until the concert. Then they pull out some little number — an orchestral transcription or a "novelty number" with a lot of cute effects, which you should have spent hours practising.

There was one time when this gruesome problem was reversed. Lois had done a fabulous recital at the University of Toronto. She was in blazing form and the audience and I were cross-eyed with adrenaline. After the usual bouquet of encores, I could see the inevitable coming.

Lois said, "Do you know Purcell's 'Hark, the Echoing Air'?"

I said that I did but that I didn't have the music.

"I brought my copy just in case," she said.

"Well, what's your tempo?"

"Just play it as fast as you can."

So on we went.

Lois's answer was in reaction to the fact that I'm better at slow than fast. What she didn't know was that I had recently played this piece for another singer's concert the week before. As I zoomed through the introduction, I saw Lois's startled expression and I smiled beatifically. Undaunted, she shot through this elaborate piece like a whirlwind and at the end threw back her head and roared with laughter. The audience loved it, but Mary Morrison, one of the principal teachers at the voice faculty, came backstage and gave me a very smart slap and said, "How dare you take the Purcell that fast."

You can't win 'em all.

Chapter 10

Drying Out and Touring with Forrester

I had been drinking fairly heavily for about fifteen years. It never bothered me — I was never falling-down drunk — and I really enjoyed it. However, there were some signs of trouble: some hints of indigestion, plus the fact that my trill at the piano — never really brilliant — was now quite mushy, suggesting that something should change. The end was quite dramatic.

The Canadian mezzo Janet Stubbs, who was having great success at the opera, asked me to do a recital with her at an important venue. She hadn't done many recitals at that point, so we worked very hard at her program. Janet had been asked if she could have only a light snack before the concert, as there was to be an "elaborate supper" after. Accordingly, we ate sparingly and then went off to the theatre for the concert.

All went well, and afterward we went to the reception, ravenously hungry.

Janet had (and still has) a stunningly beautiful figure, but the maddening thing about her is that she eats like a stevedore and never gains an ounce. (I once remarked that she ate like a horse and was rewarded with a frosty "I have a healthy enjoyment of my food.")

At the reception we were invited to help ourselves to the bar. Janet doesn't drink, so I poured myself my usual tub of gin and we mingled with the guests.

As a young girl, Janet had gone to law school, graduated, and was called to the bar before she decided to give it all up for a career in opera. At the party, there was a little man who said he had been at law school with her — she didn't remember him, but of course she was too polite to say so.

He began his remarks with "Well, Jan, I usually hate recitals by opera singers — they're so stupid, aren't they?"

There was a certain stiffening in the room. He went from there to worse, and like many gauche people he would not be distracted. I got my second gin.

There was no sign of the "elaborate supper" and the conversation was totally dominated by little Hitler. I could see that Janet's nerves were being stretched to the breaking point. Third drink.

An hour and a half went by and I was on my fourth drink by the time the hostess announced, "I am terribly sorry it's taken so long, but dinner is finally served."

She was practically mowed down by her guests as we lurched toward the dining room: Janet maddened with hunger, me with booze.

Supper consisted of creamed asparagus on toast. This was not enough. Hitler rattled on. My nerves cracked. "Oh, do shut up you dreary little bugger," I trilled. There was a wave of laughter, but I felt a cold shiver down my spine. I thought "Oh God! Janet will never speak to me again." I looked down the table and she was roaring with laughter. Janet is what used to be called a Real Lady. I've never heard a cuss-word come out of her mouth, but she loves to tell the story of the Dreary Little Bugger.

That was the end of my booze period. My trill improved considerably.

After Maureen's success with *Werther*, Opera in Concert was a going concern, so I was emboldened to ask Lois Marshall if she would do an opera for us in the third season. She jumped at the chance. When she was a child she had suffered an attack of polio, which left her with a disabling limp. This was naturally an inhibiting factor in her working in the opera. However, she loved opera, and her singing was always intensely dramatic. Her few appearances in operas staged particularly for her were always successful.

I chose Massenet's *Thérèse* as her vehicle with OIC. This rarely performed two-act opera is set during the French Revolution. The title character is an aristocratic young woman who, to protect herself, has married a member of the ruling Girondin party. When her former lover, an aristocrat himself, asks her to leave her husband and go with him into exile, she agrees. But when the Girondins are overthrown and her husband is condemned to die by the guillotine, Thérèse chooses duty over love and joins her husband on the scaffold.

This is one of Massenet's most romantic and sweeping scores, with a knockout final scene in which the heroine declaims rather than sings over a harrowing crescendo in the orchestra (the piano, of course, in our production).

I engaged an excellent cast to support Lois, including my six-year-old nephew Ben Carlson (Patsy's son) in the role of the offstage news vendor, and Lois leaped on the juicy title part with relish.

I had friends from the theatre in New York visiting at the time and they still talk about Lois's performance as one of their greatest theatrical experiences. This middle-aged woman, grasping her music stand for support, created an indelible portrait of a terrified young girl driven to desperation by the intolerable pressures of the Revolution. After her thrilling cry of *"Vive le Roi! Oh, Mort! Ouvre tes bras! Marchons!"* the audience exploded in an ovation that was never matched in my twenty years with Opera in Concert.

That season also included our first Italian opera. I have always been fascinated by *L'Amore dei tre re (The Love of the Three Kings)* by Italo Montemezzi. First performed in 1913, it enjoyed worldwide success and was given regularly until 1950 when it disappeared from the repertoire. It is a score of incomparable orchestral richness and a truly haunting melodic invention. It's impossible to get the total effect in concert — particularly with piano — but I was determined to do it. I practised the score for nearly a year. In its piano reduction the music presented innumerable problems that I was not really equipped to handle, but I persevered. I practised so hard that I gave myself bursitis in my shoulder.

I chose a great cast. Roxy sang Fiora, Paul Frey Avito, and Guillermo Silva Manfredo. After the second act, Kathy Brown, my assistant, came running backstage, saying, "Guess who's in the audience?"

I cried, "Oh, for God's sake, don't tell me. I hate knowing there is a specific person in the house."

"But you have to announce it. It's Marco Montemezzi, the composer's son." Apparently Mr. Montemezzi, who lived in Maryland, went to every performance of his father's opera, wherever it was in the world. At the end I asked him to come up and take a bow. He was charming and he was kind enough to say that it was one of the best performances of the work he had ever heard.

With the support of the four arts councils — Canada, Ontario, Metro Toronto, and Toronto — Opera in Concert was now securely launched, and I'm happy to say that it's still going strong after celebrating its thirty-fifth anniversary in the 2008–09 season.

The fourth season of Opera in Concert saw an important development. I wanted to do Mozart's *La Clemenza di Tito*. Until then, I had done only operas where there was no chorus or ones where the chorus could be cut without too much damage. The end of Act 1 of *La Clemenza* has a very dramatic effect. The chorus is offstage emitting cries of rage and horror over the attempted assassination of Tito. The chorus is essential to this powerful scene, and so I asked Kathy Brown to find me a cheap chorus. Fortunately, she had a long history of dealing with the choral scene in Toronto and she immediately suggested a small choir that had recently been formed, The Jubilate Chamber Singers. They were conducted by a man Kathy described as "a real comer," Robert Cooper.

The arrangements were made and I went with the soloists to the first rehearsal. I should have been warned by the name Jubilate Chamber Singers, because that was just what they were — a perfectly balanced chamber choir making fluty white murmurs. "Oh" and "Ah" were their only words in the opera.

I think they were somewhat startled by my rehearsal costume — full leather motorcycle drag — but that was nothing. I started working on them gently.

"How lovely. However, the dramatic situation here is *not* lovely, it's horrible."

I explained the story. "Now, let's try it again."

"Oh."

"Ah."

"No, no," I shrieked. "I want 'Ohhh! Ahhh!' Think horror, think assassination, think revolution!"

"Oh! Ah!"

"That's better," I shrilled. "Louder. Raucous! Ugly! I want you all to think as your subtext, 'They've taken my baby and bashed its brains out on the sidewalk.'"

"Ohhh! Ahhh!"

Finally.

Robert has since told me that the choir thought I was on something, but never mind, they were great at the show, and as the Opera in Concert Chorus they have been the glory of the series ever since.

In 1979, Maureen asked me to do a very strenuous tour with her — eighteen concerts in twenty-one days. The tour was sponsored by the Canada Council and the Ontario Arts Council and would take us through several small towns in northern Ontario. Maureen had done one of these tours in Saskatchewan with her long-time accompanist John Newmark, but John decided that he had done enough pioneering, so I got the job.

One of the conditions in Maureen's contracts was that she would only sing with a grand piano. Now, grand pianos don't grow on trees in northern bush country, so many of these towns had to scramble to find one.

We began in a town near the Manitoba border and worked our way back east. Maureen started her program with an aria from Handel's oratorio "Israel in Egypt." Like many of Handel's slow arias, the accompaniment consists of a series of solemn repeated chords.

I began. The chords each consisted of six notes. I played the second chord — or, I tried to. Of the six notes, four stayed down — stuck. I quickly flipped them up again — same scene. By the time the aria was over, I had spent more time flipping the keys up than I had pressing them down. The effect was decidedly odd.

During the applause, Maureen looked over at me and said through a fixed smile, "What's the matter, dear?"

"Would you like to take a look at the keyboard, dear?" Clearly, something had to be done. We appealed to the audience. A man came up and said he thought he could fix it, but that it would take a little time. Maureen floated off, saying to the audience, "We'll be back."

After about three quarters of an hour we were back and the audience good-naturedly gave us a big hand. The man hadn't been able to turn the piano into a Steinway grand, but at least most of the keys went up and down.

I said afterward, "Well, that was a trial by fire."

Maureen replied, "There's liable to be worse."

She wasn't kidding.

The pianos on that tour went from barely possible to desiccated old wrecks. At one concert Maureen said to the audience, "The piano sounds as if it has laryngitis."

She was fabulous on this tour. The drill was: do the concert, go to the reception, fall into bed, get up next morning and drive between two and three hundred miles to the next concert (Ontario is a big province!), have supper, and do the next show.

There were no concert halls up there. We played in school auditoriums, gymnasiums, town halls, churches, hockey rinks, movie houses, or wherever they could get a bunch of chairs together. Maureen treated them all as if they were Carnegie Hall. She gave 150 percent of herself at every concert, and the audiences adored her.

On tour with Maureen Forrester in northern Ontario, 1978. Maureen was tireless on this tour; I was not.

The Canada Council provided us with a coordinator who looked after the practical details and drove the car. His name was Jean Latremouille. I took to calling him Saint John because of his incredible patience and good humour. Jean was very handsome, in a 1930s movie star way, and he looked about a third of his real age, although he was only three years younger than I was. Many people said we looked somewhat alike. After one of the concerts, he and I were talking at the reception when a lady came up to me and said, "I loved your playing, and isn't it lovely that your son could travel with you?" Jean never let me forget that one.

One of the most thrilling things on the tour occurred in Huntsville, Ontario. Maureen had sung the same program there before, so she didn't want to repeat it. On her new program (she told me one time that she had eleven complete recitals at her fingertips) she had included Schumann's rather maudlin song cycle "Frauenliebe und Leben" ("Woman's Life and Love").

I have never been crazy about the piece — I remember Emmy Heim saying "What did Chamisso (the poet) and Schumann know about women? How dare they presume to write about women in that way?"

I never felt quite that strongly about it, mainly because, like all Schumann, it's a joy to play on the piano.

I was interested to see how Maureen would do it, particularly as I had recently been playing it for Lois. Lois treated the character of the woman as Everywoman and her performance had a really tragic power. When Maureen began to sing, I realized immediately that we were in a different universe. Here was a simple German girl, falling in love, getting married, having a baby, and mourning the death of her husband. Maureen was so direct, so honest, and so true in her performance that I was profoundly moved at the end and could scarcely play the beautiful postlude to the cycle.

After the last concert, Maureen, who had decided she wanted to do the driving, said as we zoomed down the highway (she never wasted any time), "Wasn't that fun? Wouldn't you like to do the same thing in Southern Ontario?"

I gulped and said, "Fine, Maureen, I'd love to."

I determined to get a new exercise routine.

The southern tour turned out to be a lot less strenuous (maybe I was in better shape). For one thing, there were only fifteen concerts in twenty-one days. The towns were also much closer together. The halls and the pianos were better, too. Maureen did the same program as up north, so we were all much more relaxed. Too relaxed as it turned out.

At one point there was a long trip between two concerts that involved a stopover in Toronto. When Jean picked me up at my home, I put the music in the back seat of the car and my bags in the trunk. Maureen drove an enormous Lincoln at that time, and she wanted to drive it for the rest of the tour. When we picked her up, Jean said "You get Madame and I'll transfer the stuff to her car."

We glided off in Maureen's chariot and drove the three hours to Blyth — the venue for that evening. We arrived at the motel in Blyth at 4:45 in the afternoon. Maureen went to her room and Jean and I went to get the bags. When I opened the trunk, I gasped. "Where's the music case?" Jean had taken the bags out of the trunk of his car and put them in Maureen's, but had neglected to see that I had left the music in the back seat.

Jean and I went to Maureen, expecting a fully justified explosion. Nothing of the sort; she immediately started making plans. She tried to get in touch with one of her four daughters who lived in Toronto, but there was no answer anywhere. I called Patsy, who was fortunately at home. I told her the situation and she immediately agreed to get the music and drive with it to Blyth. Sighs of relief all around. But then we began to calculate. Patsy lived in the northern part of Toronto and Maureen on the Lakeshore. Pat would have to drive through rush-hour traffic to get to Maureen's place and then out of Toronto. It was now 5:15 and the concert was at 8:00. Pat would never make it on time.

Maureen then phoned Raffi Armenian, at that time the conductor of the Kitchener-Waterloo Symphony. Kitchener is located about an hour and a half drive from Blyth. Yes, he had some, but not all of the music for Maureen's program. He would send it by taxi — "Should be there by 7:30," he assured us.

In the meantime, Maureen wasn't taking any chances. Right after our tour she was leaving for a tour of China with the Toronto Symphony. She was singing the twelve songs of the "Knaben Wunderhorn" by Mahler, and she had brought along the music to study on the rest of our tour. "We'll begin the program with the Mahler, if we have to," she said.

I paled. "But darling, I don't know these songs."

"Learn them, darling."

It was impossible. The damned songs are written for a huge orchestra and were never intended to be played on the piano. I buried myself in the dressing room of the theatre and started to work. I had played one or two of them before, but mostly the score was just a jungle of notes that I could barely read. I prayed for a fatal heart attack — mine or Maureen's. It got to be 7:45 — no Patsy, no taxi. Maureen breezed in looking radiant and glamorous. "How's it going, darling?" she trilled. A groan was all I could muster.

"We'll wait until 8:15 to begin and then we'll start with the songs you know, and hope that one or another of our rescuers will arrive," she pronounced helpfully.

At 8:15 we were standing in the wings, waiting to go on, and Maureen said, "You look pale, Stuart." I glanced in the mirror. I didn't recognize the death's-head looking out at me. At that moment the stage door burst open and in rushed one of Maureen's daughters waving the music case.

Pat had gone to Maureen's apartment and had been dismayed at the flat refusal of the security people to let her break in to Jean's car to retrieve the music case. At that moment, Maureen's daughter, who had the keys to Maureen's apartment, turned up, having received a message on her answering machine. After a certain amount of drama, the security guard gave in. It was decided that Maureen's daughter's car was in better shape than Pat's, so she set off, ignoring all speed limits.

And what about the taxi from Kitchener? Well, it had broken down en route, and arrived just as we were doing our last encore.

From the beginning to the end of this nightmare there was never a word of reproach from Maureen. She was going to give that full house at Blyth their money's worth — even if it was over my dead body.

Chapter 11

An Adventure with the Canadian Opera Company and a Thrilling Farewell Tour

On returning from Maureen's tour, I found a message from Lotfi Mansouri asking me to come to his office for a meeting. Lotfi had become the head of the Canadian Opera Company in 1977. I have never been comfortable dealing with The Mighty. Lotfi was very "mighty" and obviously on his way to becoming "mightier yet," as the Elgar song says. However, he was very charming, and he offered me a job.

He was planning to set up a young artists program within the COC and he asked me to be the head of it. I was delighted. I had always felt that the COC should have a resident company rather than being a mere jobbing organization, hiring different people for each opera. In Germany, there are many opera companies that have a permanent roster of artists who can call their companies home. Lotfi's idea seemed to be a step in the right direction, and I was to have the resounding title First Music Director of the Canadian Opera Company Ensemble.

The eleven singers chosen for the ensemble had already sung with Opera in Concert, so it was like being with a group of old friends. We began with high hopes.

That fall, Mother had a heart attack, and while she was in St. Michael's Hospital in Toronto, she suffered a severe stroke. Since retiring from nursing in the late sixties, she had been very happy dividing her time between her summer cottage, visiting friends in Florida during the winters, and being with me and whatever gypsies were currently passing their time at my place on Pleasant Boulevard.

Her stroke severely paralyzed her, and she probably should have died, but the people at the hospital took heroic measures and brought her back — at least enough so that she could be transferred to Riverdale

Convalescent Hospital. She received excellent care at the hospital and at the beginning I went to see her regularly. One day she asked, "When's the wedding?"

"What wedding?"

"The night nurse told me that you and she are getting married."

As I had never met the night nurse, and as I had absolutely no plans for marrying anybody, I realized that Mother was fantasizing, to put it mildly.

Very soon after, she no longer recognized me when I went to visit, so I stopped going to the hospital. I found the visits too upsetting and she didn't seem to realize whether I was there or not. Pat and Dorothy continued going and Dorothy says she thinks that Mother sometimes knew her, at least vaguely. She died peacefully in her sleep in January 1983 at the age of eighty-nine.

I had not been stellar with the job at the COC, and when my contract came up for renewal I asked John Leberg, Lotfi's assistant, for a luncheon appointment. I plunged right in.

"Lois Marshall has asked me to play her coast-to-coast farewell tour starting next fall, and I'm sure you can understand that I want to play this extended tour for one of Canada's greatest artists."

He looked relieved. Once again, I had found that I'm not a joiner or a team player. Although my real métier is as an ensemble pianist, I work best for myself, and my personality, for what it's worth, functions as a one-on-one collaborator under my own direction. Fortunately, John, Lotfi, and I have remained friends, and I left by mutual agreement. I stayed on until they could find a replacement for me, which happened at the beginning of October, just in time for me to leave with Lois on her farewell tour.

The ensemble program at the Canadian Opera Company has been in existence for over thirty years and, although it hasn't resulted in the formation of a resident company such as one still finds in Germany, it has nurtured and engaged many gifted singers who are now singing in the opera houses of the world.

In the meantime, at Opera in Concert, I had been able to realize a lifelong dream — to present a performance of Debussy's opera *Pelléas et Mélisande*. When, at my lessons with Guerrero, I hadn't prepared anything to play, our talks about art and music often focused on *Pelléas*. Guerrero told me about the profound effect the opera had on him when he first heard it in Chile. He was also a fan of Maeterlinck, the Nobel Prize–winning author on whose eponymous play the opera was based. Maeterlinck had been very much over-praised at the beginning of his career (some French critics went so far as to compare him favourably with Shakespeare) and unjustly neglected after the First World War. (There is a story that after a very opulent and elaborate performance of his play *Aglavaine et Sélysette* on Broadway in the twenties, the American actress Tallulah Bankhead growled, "There's less to this than meets the eye.") In spite of Maeterlinck's almost total neglect in the latter part of the twentieth century, Guerrero maintained that he had seen a performance of a double bill of two of Maeterlinck's one-act plays, *Les Aveugles* (*The Blind*) and *Intérieure* (*Inside*), which he said had stayed with him ever since.

Whatever the merits of Maeterlinck's dramas, *Pelléas* was exactly the type of play for which Debussy was looking as the basis for an opera. He worked on it off and on for ten years, and from the first performance, it was recognized as one of the most original and powerful of music dramas. It's certainly not for everyone. While I was doing the quiz for the CBC there was a gentleman from British Columbia who sent a number of letters complaining about my enthusiasm for it. One of the milder letters called it "tuneless drivel." Well, *chaqu'un à son drivel!*

I'm often asked what opera is my favourite and I answer Verdi's *Il Trovatore*, because, for me, opera is about singing and Verdi's melodrama affords the most stunning opportunities for great singing. But if I'm asked what my favourite music drama is, I have no hesitation in naming Debussy's one completed masterpiece.

From the beginning of my life in music, I have felt a special affinity for Debussy. I am certainly not unresponsive to the grandeurs of German music (one could hardly call oneself a musician if one were), but I have always preferred the more human scale of French music. A German musician once said to me, "Beethoven and Debussy — if one saw two boats — on the Beethoven boat there would be someone you loved who was leaving forever — the Debussy boat would be just a boat." An interesting analogy. On the other hand, how many times in your life do you see a boat in which a loved one is leaving forever and how many times, particularly if you live on a lake, as I do, do you see boats floating, balancing, gliding, about which you know nothing but their mystery?

One time when I was in Paris I went to the Opéra-Comique, where I saw a terrible performance of Massenet's *Werther*. However, it wasn't wasted time, because this was the theatre in which *Pelléas* was first performed in 1902. I was struck by the fact that the theatre was smaller than I had expected. I had only heard *Pelléas* in huge venues like the old and the new Metropolitan in New York or at the Chicago Lyric. It struck me that the small Jane Mallet Theatre, where we do Opera in Concert in Toronto, was ideal for getting across the enormous dramatic impact of this piece.

Even now, over a hundred years after its premiere, *Pelléas* is a tremendous challenge to present. I love this work so deeply that I was terrified that a performance with piano, with the artists at music stands, in evening dress, would be a travesty. Fortunately, the opposite happened. Our cast included Rosemarie Landry, whose singing of French music recalled the Golden Age, Mark DuBois at the beginning of his career, and the late great Dutch-Canadian baritone Cornelis Opthof. Learning the notes of *Pelléas* is a formidable challenge, but I was determined that the drama should speak as powerfully as the music. At that time, subtitles were in their infancy and I even made inquiries as to their feasibility for us: Impossibly expensive. So it was up to us.

After the performance, many people said to me, "I could kill myself for not knowing French — one could see that there was a tremendously powerful drama going on up there, and it was maddening not to understand every word." I said to somebody at the party after, "I don't care if I die now; I feel I've done something honourable for Debussy." Always the drama queen. This was over thirty years ago.

A few years ago, I was in Paris doing auditions for a stage director and we were in a rehearsal room at the Opéra-Comique. While the director was talking to one of the auditionees, I looked around the room. It was a very ordinary rehearsal space with practically nothing in it. But on one wall there was a small photograph.

I examined it, and there was Debussy himself rehearsing *Pelléas* with Mary Garden in this same room. Inspired by this, I ran down onto the stage and, in my most authentic Debussy style, intoned the first line of the opera — "*Je ne pourrais plus sortir de cette forêt*" — just so that I could say that I had sung *Pelléas* at the Opéra-Comique.

After making my making my *adieux* to the COC and John Leberg, Lois Marshall's Farewell Tour was a delight. She prepared three programs — a lighter program, a somewhat serious one, and a lieder evening. Interestingly enough, the more serious program was the one most requested. Possibly, people intuited that Lois was a profoundly serious artist and that's what they wanted from her. We started in Victoria on the West Coast. In Alberta, both Calgary and Lethbridge requested the *liederabend*. Lois had chosen the "Frauenliebe und Leben" of Schumann, a group of Mahler songs, and for the second half, Schumann's "Dichterliebe" — a formidable recital for any singer, let alone one making her final appearances. Lois had, for the last few seasons, been singing as a mezzo-soprano. As her career progressed, she felt more comfortable singing in the lower part of her range. Her lower voice had always been unusually rich and powerful for a soprano, so her change of register was a natural progression.

I had played all of these songs for her before, so we didn't rehearse them in the new keys; it was simply a question of me getting the new notation into my fingers. When we did the concert in Calgary, Lois had not been happy. The acoustics in the hall had been dry and she found the keys she had chosen for the songs to be too low. Could I transpose them up for the concert the next night in Lethbridge? Laugh here. (Where are you Dalton Baldwin, when I need you?)

Fortunately, at that time, Calgary had an excellent music store and I was able to obtain all the songs in the middle voice keys. We raced to Lethbridge, where I spent the afternoon getting the new keys into my fingers. Lois was happy and the Dean of Music at the university said that he had never been so moved, so we kept the middle keys.

Lois was not always at her best on this tour, but the nights she was "on" were transcendent. In Kingston, Ontario, there is a hall in which she always loved to sing. It has beautiful acoustics, and Lois had had many successful appearances there. That night she was in superb voice, and she took off like a rocket. I thought to myself, *What am I doing on stage with this woman?* She did things during that concert that I couldn't come close to matching. I said to her after, "Lois, that was overwhelming," and she replied, "Stuart, when everything works, I feel as if I am in the spheres with the composers."

The tour took us across to the East Coast, and then ended in Montreal. A few weeks later I received a present from Lois — a set of champagne glasses — with a beautiful note that is one of my treasures. It says, in part, "When I was in voice, you were there with me all the way. But on the evenings when my voice was intractable and I was struggling, I felt support from you such as I have never experienced."

With Lois Marshall at her farewell concert in Winnipeg, 1983. Lois was at her magical best.

Chapter 12

New Stars

I first met Ben Heppner in the summer of 1982, when the COC asked me to play for a two-week class being given to the members of the ensemble by the French baritone Martial Singher. I remember when Ben got up to sing "Spirto Gentil" from Donizetti's *La Favorita* that I was thrilled by the musicality and timbre of this lovely lyric tenor. But Mr. Singher would have none of it. "You are a big man, and God doesn't make monsters. You should not be singing lyric tenor, you should be singing Wagner." We all stared. "More people lose their voices by trying to sing lightly than by singing things that are heavy. If it's too heavy for you, your body will tell you soon enough." Of course Ben went on to have an international career singing thrilling performances of Tristan, Lohengrin, Siegfried, and Walter von Stolzing all over the world.

I learned a lot from those two weeks with Singher. When I met him, I told him that I had heard him sing Pelléas on the radio and saw him at the Met sing Golaud, Pelléas's brother, in the forties. "But you can't be that old!" he cried.

One day we went out for lunch. He said, "I'm not allowed to eat desserts anymore, but you have one, and I'll just take a little taste." I ordered a butterscotch sundae, which came in an enormous coupe. As soon as he saw it, Singher, who was in his eighties, grabbed it, and, singing the theme of the Presentation of the Grail from Parsifal at the top of his lungs, paraded it around the restaurant to the astonishment of the clientele.

When I finally got to eat it, he inquired, "How is the sundae?" his eyes aglow.

"Delicious."

"I'll try just a *soupçon. O la! La! C'est comme le bon Dieu descend dans la gorge, avec des culottes en velours!*" (Free translation: "It's as if the good lord was going down your throat wearing velvet pants.") With that, he took the coupe and said, "You're too fat, Stuart. I'll just finish it off!"

Ben made his debut with OIC the next season. He sang Alain in Massenet's ravishing *Grisélidis*. In later seasons, he sang Lionel in Flotow's *Martha*, Loris in Giordano's *Fedora*, and Max in Weber's *Der Freischütz* — an interesting progression, illustrating the broadening and deepening of his voice. I remember when we were rehearsing *Fedora*, he absolutely overwhelmed me with his sound, and I said, "Ben, when you sing like that, it's ridiculous you're not singing everywhere." He smiled. "My time is coming."

He wasn't kidding.

Ben rarely coached with me. He always worked with his coach and mentor, the late Dixie Ross Neill, whose husband Bill was Ben's voice teacher. However, they lived in Montreal, and occasionally when he couldn't get down to see them he would come and work with me. This was usually when he had something French to prepare. In spite of his celebrity, he is still very much the same — a very warm-hearted, open

With Ben Heppner at the Ruby Awards, October 27, 2006. Ben was awarded the Ruby in 2006. I got mine at the first awards ceremony in 2000.

sort of guy who is slightly surprised at his superstar status. I last worked with him when he was preparing for a recording of French arias. He is always fascinating to work with. Most singers will "mark" — sing half voice, or down an octave — when they're learning repertoire. Not Ben. He goes full blast for two hours at a time. The final thing he sang for me was Enée's endless and exhausting aria from Berlioz's *Les Troyens*. By the time he had finished, I was a pulverized, bubbling pool of fat on the floor. *To be in a relatively small room with that voice coming at you!*

In the fall of 1981, I got a call from John Leberg, who informed me that the COC opera productions were being picked up by the CBC under the sponsorship of Texaco. They wanted the show to resemble the broadcasts that they had been sponsoring at the Met since 1940, so they wanted a quiz at intermission. I had been listening to the Texaco broadcasts from the Met almost from the beginning, so I certainly knew the format. It turned out to be really easy. I mean, how difficult can it be to sit there with the answers and ask the questions? I did it for twenty-seven years.

In May of 1984, I received a call from a gentleman in San Luis Potosi in Mexico. Would I come to Mexico City to be a judge in the Oralia Dominguez competition? Señora Dominguez was a distinguished mezzo who had an important career in Europe and who had been born in San Luis Potosi. There would be no fee for it, but I would be flown down in a government plane, picked up in Mexico City by limousine, and driven for five hours to San Luis Potosi. Great.

The plane flew only once a week, so that would give me a couple of days to explore Mexico City before going off to the competition. The plane was two hours late leaving Toronto, however, because something had "fallen off." The rest of the journey was similarly ramshackle, but all was forgiven when I checked into a beautiful hotel in Mexico City near the fabulous archaeological museum. The museum is, of course, the jewel of this great and tragic city, and I spent a whole day there in a state of wild exhilaration.

The evening arrived for me to be picked up by the limousine. As a musician, you very early on learn to be on time, because if you're late, there's someone better than you are waiting to take your job.

Consequently, I was waiting in the hotel lobby at 6:45 for a 7:00 p.m. pickup. Seven o'clock came and went. At eight, I phoned my contact. No answer. At ten, furious, I rebooked my hotel room, went to bed, and left instructions that I was not to be disturbed until morning. In spite of this instruction the phone rang at 1:10 a.m. "Good evening, Señor Hamilton, your limousine has arrived."

I shrieked "Tell them I have retired, and that I shall be ready to leave at 9:00 a.m." With that, I pulled the telephone out of the wall and went to sleep.

Next morning, an ancient Volkswagen van wheezed up the driveway. "Señor Hamilton?" I knew it. Not a word about the previous night, and a lot of smiles.

The trip was bumpy, long, hot, and dusty. But when we finally arrived the hotel was pretty and I was introduced to my fellow judges. Herta Glaz — an Austrian mezzo whom I knew from many broadcasts from the Met in the forties — represented the U.S., a conductor from the Bellas Artes in Mexico City was the Mexican judge, and I, of course, represented Canada.

There were problems right from the start. Our Mexican colleague obviously had an agenda. He had a young friend singing in the competition who he was determined was going to win first prize. This friend was a tenor who was singing things that were far too heavy for him — particularly Otello's death scene. When Madame Glaz and I balked, the conductor accused us of being anti-Mexican. After a meeting with Madame Glaz, I blazed at the conductor. "Madame Glaz and I have come a long way and we are here as experienced musicians giving our professional opinions. We did not come here to be insulted, and if this issue is raised again, we will leave, forthwith!"

I don't think I've ever used the word *forthwith* before or since, but it seemed to do the trick.

There was a young bass in the competition who was extremely gifted. This young man had a lot of friends in the audience who were nothing if not partisan. After each number he sang there was vociferous shouting and thunderous applause. But he really *was* good, so Madame and I both felt he should win. However, this singer had worked with the conductor at one time and they hadn't got along. He said the kid was arrogant and impossible to work with. He was adamant that he should not be given first prize.

Madame Glaz phoned her friends in New York. She arranged for the young man to be flown to New York to audition for the young artists program at the Met. This was an opportunity worth much more than the prize being offered in Mexico, but when we explained this to the young man, he turned out to be just as the conductor said, and answered, "I will accept first prize, or nothing." All our pleadings had no effect, and so there was nothing to be done.

We announced the prize winners and the audience exploded with rage. They came up to the edge of the stage and shook their fists at us. I murmured to Madame Glaz, "Do you think they're going to shoot?" The demonstration went on. Something had to be done. It was suggested that I give a speech explaining our choices. Given the shaky nature of my Spanish, I demurred. It was decided that I would write something that would then be translated into Spanish, and Madame, who spoke Spanish fluently, would read it.

I hastily scribbled something about art, beauty, truth, depth, and grandeur. Madame read it like Bernhardt declaiming the Marseillaise and the audience rioted all over again — on our side this time.

I have always had ambivalent feelings about competitions. Right from my days at the Festival in Regina, I've doubted the value of reducing people and performances to numbers. Whenever possible, I've tried to get competitions where I was a judge to avoid giving marks and simply award the prizes on the merits of the performers.

I was once on a panel of judges for an international competition that was awarding large cash prizes. Several of the other judges voted down my idea of eliminating marks and, sure enough, when it came to our deliberations, one of the judges had given the competitors in one class ridiculously low marks. On examination, it turned out that one of the competitors was a pupil of his. He disqualified himself from marking her, but had given the low marks to everyone else, with the result being that she came second. We all complained, but the judge replied that that was what we had decided, and if we wanted to change the rules at this point, we would have to begin the whole competition all over again. This, as he knew, was impossible, and so the judgment stood — a manifestly unfair example of what can be done with numbers.

After this colourful but exhausting experience, I just wanted to board my "limousine" and get to the airport in Mexico City. My plane left at 7:00 the next morning and I was particularly anxious to catch it, as I had a concert to play in Toronto the following night. However, the governor of the province — a charming man, by the way — insisted I come to the reception for "just one drink." At 11:00 p.m. I convinced them to let me go back to the hotel to pack and meet my driver.

The "limousine" this time looked like a reject from the Beverly Hillbillies — a pickup truck with a huge load of live chickens in the back. The driver spoke no English, but was very affable, so off we chugged. He was very prudent — he never went above thirty-five miles per hour. I'm not sure the truck *could* go any faster, but my urgings drew no response anyway, so I settled down.

Five miles out of town, the driver put on a tape of a type of Mexican music that seemed to be mainly trumpets and a chorus shrieking in falsetto like a bunch of mice in a cartoon. And it was loud. I tried to get him to turn it down, but that, too, brought no response. I considered ripping the bloody machine out by its roots, but he was a lot bigger than I was. Besides, he obviously loved it and occasionally would join in as loud as he could.

Mexico is a southern country, right? This was the latter part of May and so I had brought what I figured to be the appropriate outfits for a tropical spring. But I hadn't considered the lunar cold of the desert at night, and I was freezing in my frail silk suit. Of course, the truck had no heater. And then the chickens started to wake up. They seemed to have a lot to talk about and they added their racket to the mice screaming on the tape.

The truck chugged, I froze, the music howled, the chickens squawked. I thought to myself, *If there is a hell, this is it.*

Speedy Gonzales made many pit stops along the way, often having a leisurely coffee as well. What was left of my nervous system began to get jumpy. When we finally steamed into the suburbs of Mexico City, I saw a clock in a store window. It said 5:45. Trying to control my panic, I got across that we should go faster, or I was going to miss my plane. The only problem was that we were now in the city and so a traffic cop stopped us for speeding. Nothing happens quickly in Mexico, so the driver and the cop had a long, loud discussion about the ticket. I was gnashing my teeth, trying to console myself with the fact that the plane *had* been two hours late leaving Toronto.

The driver pointed triumphantly to his watch as we pulled up to the terminal. Seven o'clock, right on the nose. I rushed to the gate. "But señor, the plane left at 7:00."

"But it was late leaving Toronto."

"Señor, our planes are never late."

"Well, what am I going to do?"

"This ticket is only good on this flight. It goes again in a week. Come back then and be on time."

I phoned the office at the competition in San Luis Potosi and was told they had gone out of business the day before. I had to buy a one-way ticket to Toronto (actually Dallas, change, Chicago, change, *then* Toronto) which cost me $950. I sent the receipt to the Oralia Dominguez competition people, but I never heard from them again.

A few weeks later, Lotfi Mansouri asked me, "How was that competition in Mexico? They asked me to go, but I was busy, so I suggested you for the job."

Thanks a lot, Lotfi!

That spring, we celebrated the completion of our tenth season of Opera in Concert. In our first ten years we had presented 154 artists in forty operas. Under Carrol Anne's instigation, many of these artists contributed to buying and presenting me with a beautiful score of Massenet's *Manon*, published in 1884, the year of the opera's premiere. As if this weren't enough, the score is autographed and has a handwritten quote from the opera by Massenet himself.

The opera we performed that evening was Thomas's *Mignon*, and with the title role, Carrol Anne sang her last part with Opera in Concert. Later that year she gave up her singing career to join the Canada Council as a Music Officer. Eventually she left the council and became the head of the classical division of Dean Artists Management. She is now what I kid her as being the "most powerful woman in music in Canada." (Tremble.) I'm also happy to say that she is one of my very closest and dearest friends.

By the age of fifty-five, I had begun to "bulk up," as the guys say (actually, I was just getting fat), so I decided that I was butch enough at that point to attempt the YMCA as an exercise venue. Their old building, where I had stayed for that stressful week in 1948, had recently been torn down and replaced with a beautiful new structure two blocks from my apartment.

I presented myself for a test to see the level at which I should begin. The test was administered by a bright young lady who said perkily, "Well, Mr. Hamilton, we call your body type Fatty-Sleepy. Now, it's very difficult for Fatty-Sleepies to exercise, but very, very important. So get in there, Fatty-Sleepy, and get going." I considered slamming her head against the wall, but thought better of it. She was probably tougher than I was.

The Y was a culture shock. The building is beautifully maintained and immaculately clean. But the noise. The blaring music. The exotic scents. I had dropped into another world. After a few weeks, I began to run into the same people. I would say, brightly, "Good morning," or "Hi." The ladies would reply, but the guys would look at me like a deer caught in the headlights, mumble something, then turn away. I finally discerned that they were saying "Hardoon!" It was easy enough, but what did it mean? *Hardoon.* I went along with it and it worked wonders. All the guys spoke to me and I began to relax. Eventually, I got up enough nerve to ask a pal with whom I had begun a casual friendship, "What the hell does *hardoon* mean?"

"Oh, you crazy thing. They're saying 'How are you doing?'" The lingo is all important.

On December 19, 1984, I was coaching the beautiful mezzo-soprano Deborah Milsom, who sang many leading roles with OIC. During a break in the lesson, I opened the mail. "Oh, Deb," I gasped, "I've been made a Member of the Order of Canada." She ran across the studio to kiss me, "Darling, what a wonderful honour. Does this mean we get to call you Dame Stuart?"

She was right about one thing. It *is* a great honour and very moving to be recognized by your fellow citizens. One of the conditions of the Order is that you phone them to tell them of your acceptance. Of course, I called the next day, and I couldn't resist a little levity. I asked the gentleman if I could have the medal made so that I could wear it in my nose (nose rings were just coming in). There was a glacial pause.

"In your nose?"

"Yes, I'm very proud of it, and I want everyone to know. Ha!"

"Oh. I see ... a joke."

I would never have made it in the political world.

The presentation ceremony took place the following April at Rideau Hall, the official residence of the governor general of Canada. There had been a huge snowfall all that day and my guest, Kathy Brown from OIC, and I were nearly late arriving.

I have never much liked hair. I have always had what other people described as beautiful hair — which essentially means there's a lot of it. But it's always been a big drag to look after, so I decided for the ceremony to shave my head. This is all very well if you have a nicely shaped head, like, for instance, Lotfi Mansouri (who has, as long as I've known him, been as bald as a bean). But my head turns out to be really funny looking. It comes to a sort of ridge in the middle from which it falls away, on one side round and the other side flat. Add to this the fact that I have a large, previously undetected Gorbachev birthmark on the back of my head, and you have something other than the effect for which I was hoping.

The governor general, the late Jeanne Sauvé, gave two very moving speeches (one in English and a different one in French) on the meaning of the Order's motto — *Desiderantes meliorem patriam* ("They wish for a better homeland"). Then the recipients are called individually to receive their medals. As I was walking up the aisle, I saw Maureen sitting on the guest side. At that time she headed up the Canada Council, and she was there in her official capacity (she had received the Order of Canada at its initial séance in 1967). I hadn't seen her in some time, and when I walked past in all my bald splendour, I heard her say, in a rather more projected voice than absolutely necessary, "Oh, for God's sake."

Somewhat unnerved, I took my place before Madame Sauvé to receive my medal. As you stand there, they read your citation. This was a little gruesome, as the other citations said things like "You have discovered the cure for such and such" or "You have contributed to the welfare of so and so." Mine said "You have presented a lot of unknown operas." But I didn't care, I was there, and I got my medal, and it was one of the proudest moments of my life. Afterward, Maureen came over and said, "Well, your head looks like a pig's ass!"

Later, Lotfi got me in a corner and said, "Okay, I want to know the real reason you shaved your head."

I purred, "I call it 'Homage à Lotfi.'"

He didn't look convinced.

Receiving my Membership of the Order of Canada in 1985. Anne Murray and Oscar Peterson, who were made Companions of the Order the same year, are seated in the front row.

In the summer of 1987, I attended a performance of *Ariadne auf Naxos* at the Banff School of Fine Arts. I was sitting in the theatre in the benevolently somnolent state that Strauss's astonishing mixture of stupefying virtuosity, banality, and occasional sublimity always produces in me. Suddenly I woke up. Something extraordinary was happening. There was a rather rotund but hunky young man being very funny as the

Dance-Master and out of whom was coming an amazing sound. The role is short, but he eclipsed everyone else in the opera.

I scrambled for my program and found a name that meant nothing to me: Richard Margison.

I went backstage to seek him out. He was very guarded and obviously shy. I asked him about his availability to sing in Toronto. He was evasive, but at least I got his address. As soon as I got home, I wrote to him to see if he had any plans for coming to Toronto. (OIC could never afford travel expenses for out-of-town artists.) He replied that he might be available in March of 1988. I immediately offered him the role of Nangis in Chabrier's enormous operetta *Le Roi Malgré Lui*.

He accepted.

He arrived a few days before the performances and I found his voice had grown remarkably since I had heard him last. He sailed through the very tricky role with great élan.

Le Roi Malgré Lui is one of the most tremendous scores I know. Lois Marshall said after the show, "There's enough music in that piece for ten operas." The score nearly killed me to learn, but the performance was terrific and Richard created a sensation. I immediately engaged him for the next season.

With Richard Margison in his dressing room at the Metropolitan Opera after his highly successful debut as Pinkerton in Puccini's *Madama Butterfly*, 1998.

He was also engaged by the COC. His roles with them over the years tell an interesting story. Vitek in *The Makropulos Case* by Leoš Janáček, a character role; the Italian Singer in *Der Rosenkavalier* by Strauss, a small role demanding a first-class tenor; Tito in Mozart's *La Clemenza di Tito* (he had sung most of the Mozart tenor roles previously); Rudolfo in Puccini's *La Bohème* (one of the summits of the tenor repertoire); and Manrico in Verdi's *Il Trovatore*, in which by that time he had already triumphed at the Met. In other words, in an incredibly short period his was a journey from character tenor to international lyric spinto. (A spinto tenor is one who sings the heaviest roles in the French and Italian repertoire.)

And he is still developing. At one lesson he asked me about singing Bacchus in Strauss's *Ariadne auf Naxos*. I reeled. "Not on your life. It's twelve minutes of hell for the tenor."

He ignored my advice and went on to have one of his greatest successes at the Met singing it opposite Natalie Dessay and Deborah Voigt. By 2008, he was singing the lyric German repertoire around the world. His performance of Florestan in the COC's 2009 production of *Fidelio* was a revelation.

The same thing happened at OIC. Nangis is a lyric tenor part. The next role I offered Richard was Gualtiero in Bellini's beautiful *Il Pirata*. By the time he came to sing it, his voice had changed entirely. It was no longer a silvery, slender sound, but a full-throated, powerful, and gleaming one. *Il Pirata* was too light for Richard at that point.

He later described his performance as a "struggle with strangulation," but you would never have known it; the audience was electrified. The show was a terrific success, with a cast that included the stunning Stephanie Bogle, who always gave her leading men a run for their money, Michael Schade, and John Fanning, both of whom went on to sing at the Met.

Having learned my lesson, I next offered Richard Rodrigue in Massenet's *Le Cid* — a full-blown spinto role. Alas, by the time we got around to doing *Le Cid*, Richard was singing everywhere and couldn't work it into his schedule. However, he did return for my last season to do a benefit for us, which made the company a lot of money.

Every singer has his or her own particular spark of individuality; finding that spark is always a terrific thrill, but I would have to say that for sheer visceral punch, I know of no one who compares with Richard.

Opera in Concert added an orchestra for one of its presentations each season starting in 1986. This was an expensive step, but at this time we were being generously supported by businessmen John Adamson and George Paech, as well as the continuing subsidies from the Jackman Foundation and the four arts councils.

Our first orchestral opera was Donizetti's *La Favorita* and the next season Roxy did her last appearance with us in a gala Russian program. This was a great event. Roxy sang scenes from Shostakovich's *Lady Macbeth of Mtzensk*, Rimsky's *The Tsar's Bride*, and, most movingly, the letter scene from *Eugene Onegin* by Tchaikovsky. After intermission, we did the second act of Borodin's *Prince Igor*. Robert conducted with tremendous flair and the chorus had a field day with the Polovtsian Dances. There were some Soviet politicians visiting Toronto at the time, and they came backstage to congratulate everyone on their Russian diction. I didn't bother to tell them that our Russian diction coach — a wonderful woman named Vera Kaushansky — was a refugee from the Soviet Union.

Roxy has gone on to be a highly respected singing teacher and to head up the voice department of the Glenn Gould School at the Royal Conservatory of Music in Toronto for many years.

Later seasons brought Paul Frey back from Europe (he actually arrived from San Francisco, where he had been singing his signature role, Lohengrin. This role is one which, incidentally, he has sung more times than any other tenor in the history of the Wagner Festival in Bayreuth). He sang an exciting *Samson et Dalila* and Ben Heppner — already an international star — sang Max in *Der Freischütz*.

In 1988, Lois Marshall won the Toronto Arts Award in the music division. I presented the award to her, and when the directors of the awards asked to see me the next year, I assumed it was to present again. I was really surprised when they said that I had myself had been given the award for the performing arts section. Accompanists are not usually honoured in this way. Maureen presented me with my medal, bringing down the house with her story of my "pig's ass" hairdo of five years before. (My hair was back. One of the guys at the Y said "When are you getting your hair cut, Hamilton? You're beginning to look like Lana Turner." Well, I have always loved Lana.)

Part of the Toronto Arts Award is that you get to commission a work from another artist. Opera in Concert had never had enough money to have a logo designed, so I asked my friend David Deveau, who had been a graphic artist, to suggest someone in the field to come up with something distinctive. I was really happy with the result, which OIC is still using, by the way, but there was a certain amount of criticism in the Toronto art community that a logo was not a work of art. Fortunately, the TAA directors were delighted to have a piece of graphic art included in their commissions, so all ended happily.

In 1988, Matt Hughes, the head of the piano department at Acadia University in Nova Scotia, decided to set up a summer opera school with the aim of developing it into a professional opera company for the Maritimes. The four Maritime provinces were the only ones in Canada where an opera company was still lacking. To help him get it going, he called on his fellow alumnae from the University of Texas, Bill Neill, and his late wife Dixie, the coach who had taken over my old job with the COC, and had successfully run the program since.

Their first summer was very satisfying for everyone and they asked me to come and coach the second summer.

My feelings of inadequacy always assail me when I am starting a new job. I had never worked with Bill and Dixie but I knew them to be very high-powered people. They turned out to be great colleagues and I loved working at the school. Matt and his partner Roger Johnson have since become two of my best friends.

I was asked back for the next two summers, the second one being a celebration of Mozart's bicentennial. Poor Mozart was being played to death in 1991, so I conceived the idea of a concert performance of Massenet's *Thaïs* to celebrate. Unfortunately, money problems arose and the whole thing collapsed after the 1990 term. It's taken nearly a decade before there has been even a stirring of professional opera in the Maritimes since.

Chapter 13

A Problem, and More New Stars

In 1989, I noticed that there was something wrong with my right hand. I could no longer straighten out my fifth finger. The doctor told me that I was suffering from Dupuytren's contracture, a condition particularly prevalent among Celtic people over fifty who drink. It's sometimes called "Irishman's Finger." (Baron Guillaume Dupuytren was a celebrated surgeon in early nineteenth-century Paris and he discovered this condition — or at least the condition is identified with his work on it. I had come across his name several times while reading Balzac's *La Comédie Humaine*.)

The condition in my case was severe, and would require surgery and a lengthy period of post-operative inactivity.

I had to finish out the season with OIC — Barber's *Vanessa* and Gounod's *Mireille*. By the time they came along, my fourth finger was beginning to go down as well, so I played those operas with eight fingers instead of ten. One of my friends said afterward, "It didn't matter, darling. It was no worse with eight fingers than with ten." While my right hand was out of action, I learned Ravel's *Concerto for the Left Hand*, a terrific piece that I could never play in public, but which kept me sane.

The recovery period is usually six weeks to two months, but as soon as the stitches (thirty-two of them) were out, I started practising. When I had my post-operative examination three weeks later, the doctor and his gang of interns were astounded at my recovery. As I explained, "Listen guys, it's either move those fingers or try to sell my body on the streets, and at sixty, that's not much of a choice."

I could see that the energy level I needed for running OIC was not going to last forever. It was clear that I must look for a general manager to whom I could eventually turn over the company. Kathy Brown, after having been my right hand for sixteen seasons, left to pursue other goals, so the need was pressing. Doing Opera in Concert was tremendously satisfying, but choosing the operas, casting them with two casts, rehearsing them, and then driving the performances is obviously for a younger man. During my tenure as artistic director of the company I did over a hundred performances of more than fifty operas, but by the sixteenth season, I was beginning to feel my age.

Guillermo Silva-Marin had been a mainstay of the company since the first opera, *Hamlet*, in 1974. He had had a long career as a baritone and later as a tenor. He had established a very successful summer opera program (the Summer Opera Lyric Theatre) for young singers in Toronto in 1985 and brilliantly managed the chaotic problems of the Toronto Operetta Theatre, which he founded in 1986.

He coached with me for years and we had become great friends; he began as general manager for the 1990–91 season.

For my last season with OIC in 1993–94, I conceived the plan to repeat the three operas of the first season — *Hamlet*, *Béatrice et Bénédict*, and *Thaïs* — but this time all with full orchestra. However, the economic world was contracting in 1993 and we were not in a position to afford three orchestral performances.

We began the season with a gala performance of *Hamlet*, with Robert Cooper conducting the orchestra. This was performed in the huge, decrepit, but beautiful-sounding Massey Hall. It was picked up by the CBC and broadcast on *Saturday Afternoon at the Opera*. I scored a great coup by obtaining the beloved and charismatic Canadian mezzo Judith Forst for Gertrude and our old friend and super reliable Peter Barcza as Hamlet. For Ophelia, we had the very young and gifted Jacalyn Short. Jackie has since gone on to establish herself as one of Canada's busiest sopranos, but this was her first big assignment. Just before the Mad Scene, she had some sort of indisposition and there was chaos backstage. Judith, who was in the midst of a fabulous performance herself, knew exactly what to do. She pulled Jackie's head back and poured a whole can of Coca-Cola down her throat and Jackie revived immediately. Her performance of the Mad Scene was a bit wired, but it brought down the house.

The only show I played that season, and my last as artistic director, was Delibes's *Lakmé*. Everything went well until ten minutes before the end of the second performance, when the lights went out. The audience, which probably thought that this was part of the show, was dead quiet. I intoned into the black, "I realize I'm only running this company for another ten minutes, but I really can't do it in the dark. Is someone trying to tell me something?" The lights came back on, the audience roared; we made it to the end, and twenty years of happy servitude were over.

It was time for me to go, but I did feel a little bit like the rat leaving the sinking ship. During the time I ran OIC we never had a deficit and we even had a small endowment. But in 1994, it wasn't hard to see that this was about to change. The price of everything increased (does it ever decrease?) and money was getting tighter. The worst thing was that the funding from the arts councils was being cut back — particularly in Ontario.

I think everyone concerned realizes how important Opera in Concert has been to the musical life of Toronto. There is no question that it has had its part in the explosion of Canadian singers singing internationally today. Bill has worked like a demon since I left and he has had many artistic successes, particularly in the ravishing series of Handel operas he has presented. I'm very proud of Opera in Concert, but I'm very glad that I don't run it anymore.

I had made certain commitments to several singers, so Bill asked me to do the first opera of his regime — Bellini's *I Capuleti e I Montecchi*. He asked me again for the next season and I agreed to do one last show. At Opera East, in Nova Scotia, I had tried an experiment that had worked very well. We did Massenet's one-act opera *Le Portrait de Manon* (a sequel to his *Manon*) preceded by the scenes and arias from *Manon*, which are quoted in *Le Portrait*. I told Bill I would do this if he could get me Russell Braun for the role of Des Grieux in the *Portrait*. Russell had started in the chorus of OIC, progressed through supporting roles, and in 1992 had triumphed in the leading role of Don Pedro in Donizetti's *Maria Padilla*. His big aria in the opera signalled the arrival of a major star, and by the applause when he finished it, it was clear that the audience was thrilled to be in on his emergence. By 1994 he was well on his way to the stardom he now enjoys in Salzburg, the Bastille in Paris, and the Met. In 2001 he won the Dora Award in Toronto for his incandescent performance of Billy Budd with the COC. Fortunately, he was available, and so I definitely ended my association with the OIC on the highest level.

Le Portrait de Manon was the thirteenth opera of Massenet that I did for the company. People have often asked me, "Why this reliance on a composer so out of fashion, if not out of date?"

There are many reasons. For one thing, Massenet loved singers and he knew how to write beautifully for the voice. In Opera in Concert we were in the main dealing with young voices, and Massenet is kinder for young singers than the great German or Italian composers. Massenet is not a great composer in the way Mozart, Wagner, or Verdi are great. If you have the talent to raise yourself to their level, you will have great performances because of the blazing genius of the material. Massenet, on the other hand, offers the singer a delicious blueprint for the imagination and personality of the artist to display itself. When a Massenet opera is carefully prepared and presented, it always works for the audience. It certainly did for our purposes.

Shortly after my retirement from OIC, my longtime colleague Jean MacPhail sent me one of her pupils for coaching. When this girl made her appointment on the phone she gave me her name. It was so long that I gave up and simply wrote in my appointment book "Isabelle." She turned out to be a stunningly beautiful Armenian girl with enormous Byzantine eyes. She glanced at my book and said, "You spelled my name wrong. It's I-S-A-B-E-L, not I-S-A-B-E-L-L-E."

"Well," I laughed, "that shortens it a little bit. I'll never be able to manage your last name. It goes on forever."

She was not amused. "It's a perfectly simple name, *Bayrakdarian*. You'll get it if you concentrate a bit."

Slightly nonplussed by all this cool, I asked her to sing. She had a nice voice, but something was wrong. She was singing as a mezzo-soprano, and although I've never been very good at hearing what voice a singer should be using, I felt that she was definitely a soprano. (I once told the American soprano Karan Armstrong that she should never sing Strauss's Salomé, that it was far too heavy for her voice. She ignored my advice and went on to become one of the most celebrated Salomés of her time. Mind you, Karan had a gorgeous figure, and when she danced the Dance of the Seven Veils she took off *all* her clothes, so that might have had something to do with her success.)

When I told Isabel about being a soprano, she simply said, "I'll talk it over with my teacher." Period.

As we went on with our coaching, I gradually began to learn a little more about her. She had recently arrived in Canada from Lebanon, where she had been born. She was studying at the University of Toronto — bio-medical engineering, whatever that was. (I later discovered that it is one of the toughest courses in science.) When I asked her what she hoped to do with her singing, she replied simply, "In ten years, I'll be at the Met."

I smiled. "Now, Isabel, don't you think you should concentrate on your university studies, and when you've got your degree, *then* work on your voice?"

"Oh, if I didn't have my singing, I'd go crazy. I can do them both."

After about a year of this, whatever condescension I may have felt began to melt away. One day (now a soprano) she asked me to suggest a French aria for her. "It's for the finals of the Met competition."

I gawked. "What Met competition?"

"Well, I won all the preliminaries and I'm in the finals in New York. They say I should have a French aria. Which one should I sing?"

"But Isabel, *darling*, when are the finals?"

"Next week."

After I picked myself off the floor, I said, "But why didn't you tell me about all this?"

"I didn't want to bother you about it. What French aria should I sing?"

I thrashed around for a minute and came up with Manon's "Adieu, notre petite table." I said, "It's not too difficult to learn, but you'll have to come and coach it. It's a very subtle piece."

She came back in a couple of days with it memorized. But what was really astounding was that she sang it with real psychological penetration. This was beginning to be creepy.

I gave her a few ideas and sent her off. Of course, she won. Not being satisfied with having her first professional experience on the stage of the Metropolitan Opera, the Armenian archbishop felt she should make her recital debut at Carnegie Hall. She called me. "Can you come down to New York and play a recital for me next week?"

"Sure, Isabel." And so I did.

On her program, she sang several Armenian songs, and as the sold-out house consisted mostly of Armenians, this group was a huge success. Before the group, Isabel complained that they were a tough audience.

"What do you mean, a tough audience?" I exclaimed. "Listen to them. They're cheering."

"Yes," she admitted, "but I had to *make* them cheer."

With Isabel Bayrakdarian at the Carnegie Recital Hall, New York, March 1997. This was a very last-minute affair, but Isabel knocked them dead.

At the reception after the concert, the archbishop, a charming and cultivated gentleman, expressed surprise that I, as an obviously non-Armenian, played the songs so expressively, which gave me a chance to go into my "music has no boundaries" routine, which he said he found quite moving.

This astonishingly gifted young woman made her Metropolitan Opera debut in a leading role in William Bolcom's *A View from the Bridge* in 2002 — a year ahead of her schedule. What's more, she graduated as a biomedical engineer at the head of her class.

In 2000, the magazine *Opera Canada* inaugurated a series of annual awards in honour of the late Ruby Mercer, the founder of the magazine. Maureen Forrester won for Performance and I for Opera Educator. The event was very gala and it was held at the Granite Club. Jon Vickers was the presenter. One thing about Jon: when he talks, you listen. It was rather like getting an award from the prophet Elijah. The somewhat solemn evening was brought to a hilarious close when Jackie Short, dressed in a leather outfit that wouldn't have looked out of place in a porn magazine, serenaded me with my least favourite aria, "Una voce poco fà," from Rossini's *Barber of Seville*, but with very special, racy lyrics written by her and her husband, Michael Cavanagh. Jackie was fabulous and everybody left with huge smiles on their faces.

Chapter 14

Broadcasting and Winding Down

The executive producer of the show *Saturday Afternoon at the Opera* (*SAATO*) for the CBC was none other than the choirmaster of Opera in Concert, Robert Cooper. (If you're an artist in Canada, you have to wear many hats.) So we had an interesting situation. Robert was my boss at CBC, and I was his at OIC. I was delighted with the work Robert was doing with the chorus of OIC. Things at the CBC took a little longer to settle down.

Robert is a magnificent choral conductor and a man of phenomenal energy. Like many talented people, he is also high-strung. When I began to do the quiz and intermission features in the studio I was very nervous, especially if, in addition to announcing the feature, I had also written it. I knew that Robert wanted me to do well, but that only added to the tension. Often, I would get about three minutes into the feature and my voice would start to get watery. I would say to myself, *Come on, you jerk, you've been telling people how to deal with their voices for years. Now get that diaphragm down.*

No use. Robert would come on the speaker and say, "Stuart, are you about to have a heart attack?" I didn't know how to tell Robert that his intensity, which was practically melting the glass between the control booth and the studio, was part of the problem. One time, he was particularly stressed.

"Okay, Stuart. Are you ready?" he rasped.

"I think so, Robert."

"No, no. You have to be sure."

"I'm sure, Robert."

"All right, I'm rolling the tape."

"Okay, Robert."

"Now, Stuart, don't fuck up."

This was obviously good advice, but not exactly what was needed at that moment. Actually, it became a great joke around the CBC and Robert and I have had many laughs about it since.

We had a little talk. I explained to him that I don't respond to that kind of pressure, so it was decided that I would do only the occasional feature and simply continue as the quizmaster. Also, as the executive producer, Robert got someone else to produce the quiz itself. Everything was solved and both Robert and I celebrated our twenty-fifth anniversary with *SAATO* in 2007.

My work with CBC was a great joy. We really had a terrific team at *SAATO*. The *éminence grise* was, of course, Robert, and it was no accident that he was the producer of the two most popular shows on CBC Radio 2. Our host, Howard Dyck, was the consummate pro. I was lost in admiration for the way he could read page after page of complicated script without turning a hair.

There were many wonderful moments in my nearly twenty-seven years on the program, but probably the greatest happened on November 2, 1996. Robert had the superb idea to celebrate the sixtieth anniversary of CBC Radio with a retrospective look at the CBC Opera Company, which had existed from 1948 to 1957.

A capacity house filled the Glenn Gould Studio to overflowing and the atmosphere was electric. The script was, as always, by our own brilliant Warren Wilson, and Carrol Anne Curry, who did the Opera Update segment of the show, was on hand to interview Ruby Mercer, out of whose show, *Opera Time*, *SAATO* had developed. My job was to interview as many of the singers as we could find from the original broadcasts of the CBC Opera Company.

And we found many of them, including June Kowalchuk, Mary Morrison, Barbara Franklin, Joan Hall, Mary Simmons, Jan Rubes, Elizabeth Benson Guy, Glen Gardner, Patricia Snell, Patricia Rideout, Lois Marshall, and Jon Vickers — a true galaxy of magnificent Canadian stars. During the show, we played excerpts from the various operas in which they had sung.

Lois was adorable on the show. She got a huge laugh when she said, "I am horrified to realize that I am twelve years older than the CBC." Jon looked magnificent and was absolutely charming and very gallant with the ladies with whom he had sung. It was a fabulous afternoon and my glow over its memory is only clouded by the fact that this was the last time I saw Lois. She died three months later.

Much as I enjoy broadcasting, there can be drawbacks. A few seasons ago, I was on the panel of *The Quiz* for the broadcast of *La Traviata* from the Metropolitan Opera in New York. There was a great snowstorm that weekend, so instead of indulging in one of New York's gourmet restaurants after the opera, I struggled back through the drifts and had supper in the little dining room at the hotel. I was early, so the maitre d' said, "Because of the storm, we don't have many reservations for this evening, so I can give you our best table, right at the window."

The view of Central Park covered with the sparkling, fresh snow was indeed lovely. I ordered supper and settled back with a glass of champagne.

"That man is in my seat!"

I felt like L.R. Riding Hood at the home of the three bears.

"But Madam," murmured the maitre-d', "I have a lovely table right here from which you have an even more beautiful view."

"But I want my regular table."

I thought for a moment of giving up my table, but then I thought, *Oh, really! That's too Canadian. This is New York, after all!* and I turned my back and continued to admire the view.

Connie (not her real name) finally settled down at her unaccustomed spot, but I knew what was coming. "What kind of a haircut is that?" she shrilled. (I wear my hair very short.) "And what in the world is that outfit?" (Leather drag) "You're weird."

I allowed that, yes, I was very weird.

"Where are you from?"

"I'm from Canada."

"Canada! I've never known anybody from Canada. I'm from California." (The inference being that if you're from California, you are exempted from knowing anyone from Canada.)

She continued. "I'm here on an opera tour. I've seen four operas so far: *Il Trovatore*, *Fidelio*, *La Traviata*, and *Die Fledermaus*. The only one I liked was *La Traviata* — all the others take place in a prison. I like operas to look pretty. I suppose you don't like opera," she said with a sneer.

"Actually, I *do* like opera. I was at *La Traviata* this afternoon."

"Wasn't it lovely? Ruth Anne is from California." — Ms. Swenson, who sang the leading role is actually a native of New York, but perhaps she lives in California — "We're all very proud of her. I don't suppose you have any opera singers in Canada."

My voice became almost as raucous as hers. "As a matter of fact, we have many magnificent opera singers in Canada. The man whom you saw singing the leading role so superbly in *Fidelio* is Canadian, and we're all very proud of *him*."

"Is that so? I couldn't see him; it was so dark in that stupid jail."

It must have been really dark. Ben Heppner is not that difficult to see.

At this point the very distinguished-looking gentleman at the next table turned around and said, "Excuse me, but aren't you Stuart Hamilton? I'm Peter Allen."

I leaped out of my chair to shake his hand.

"Oh, Mr. Allen, I'm so delighted to meet you. You've been announcing my name on the Met broadcasts for ten years and I've never laid eyes on you." (The broadcast booth at the Met and the small theatre where they do *The Quiz* are in different venues.)

He introduced me to his chic wife, and we were chatting politely when "Connie" shrieked, "Who are you talking to there?"

"This is Mr. Peter Allen."

"Never heard of him."

"But you must have. Mr. Allen announces the Metropolitan broadcasts."

"I hate opera on the radio. I can never tell where we are in the story."

"You must have heard some of the broadcasts."

"Well, when my husband was alive, he listened to them all the time."

"Then you must have heard this gentleman. He announces the broadcasts."

"You mean this is Milton Cross?"

Mr. Allen doubled up.

"No, no," I exclaimed. "Milton Cross died twenty-five years ago. This is Peter Allen."

"Never heard of you. But how do you do."

"*Sic transit gloria,*" I murmured to Mr. Allen.

At this point, the waiter, whose name was Abraham, brought my dinner. Connie rasped, "Is that Abraham as in Lincoln, or Abraham as in the bible?"

"I am Palestinian, Madam."

"Palestinian! The trouble with you people is that you can't get along with the Jews. What's the matter with you?"

I looked at Abraham and raised my eyes to heaven as if to say *I'm a Canadian, you know, Abe!*

"Have you ever been to Jerusalem, Madam?" he asked.

"Yes, I was there on a tour once."

"Well, didn't you think it was the most beautiful city?"

"It was all right."

"But didn't you feel that the very stones were holy?"

"Oh, don't hand me that — I'm an atheist."

Abraham retreated.

Enter two handsome young men who went up to her table and said, "How's it going, Connie?" It turned out they were the managers of the opera tour.

"Not bad," she allowed, "except this weirdo has my table."

They glanced at me.

"Oh, my God! You're Stuart Hamilton. We were at *The Quiz* this afternoon. You were wonderful."

Connie yelled, "What is this — are you somebody?"

"No, no. I'm nobody."

"Don't you believe it, Connie. He was the star."

"Well, if you're some star or something, I have to have your name so I can tell my friends. What's your name?"

"Stuart Hamilton."

How do you spell that? S-t-e-w-"

"No, no, s-t-u-a-r-t."

"That's a stupid way to spell it."

"It was good enough for Mary, Queen of Scots."

"You some sort of queen?"

"Uh, well—"

Totally vanquished, I left Abraham a huge tip and stumbled back to my room.

I loved the three producers with whom I have worked on the quiz for
SAATO, Lawrence Beckwith (son of John), Alison Howard (a very lovely
and classy lady with whom I discovered I shared Helen Dahlstrom as a
teacher — mind you, Alison studied with her forty years after I did), and
Jurgen Petrenko.

The only problem was that Jurgen had been an organist. I would walk
a million miles to avoid hearing an organ. For me, organists sound like
they're sitting on the keyboard. The sound never stops. The music never
seems to be taking a breath.

Once when I was in Hamilton I went to an organ recital that was
inaugurating an antiphonal organ in a church where one of my pupils was
the soloist. They had a guest organist from England and, to show what the
organ could do, he played a piece called "The Chimes of Westminster."
The racket at the end of this long and tiresome showpiece was really
deafening, and when the noise finally stopped, in the dead silence that
followed, a little boy yelled out, "Ouch!" He expressed my feelings exactly.

I told this story to Jurgen and, although he turned out to be great fun
and a wonderful colleague, he was not amused.

Doing the quiz was very satisfying. I've met many people who have
told me that they didn't always listen to the whole opera but they never
missed the quiz. On the last broadcast of the season of 2007, I announced
that "God willin' and the crick don' rise, we'll be back next spring." Well,
the crick rose and we were all drowned in it! Robert was the first to go.
He took Carrol Anne and me out for a glamorous lunch and said that
the signs for going on were not good. However, I never received any
official notice and the 2008 season started without a quiz. Three weeks
into the season, I got a call from Robert's replacement, who said, "You're
fired." So, after twenty-seven years, that was the end of my career with
the CBC.

Later, I received a beautiful letter from Robert that said, in part, "you
were the unquestionable star of *Saturday Afternoon at the Opera* — and I
can never fully thank you for all you brought to the program. — I carry
with me the daily awareness of your gracious, urbane, gentle, open, honest,
sincere and generous person."

As Anna Russell so memorably said in her hilarious lecture on Wagner's Ring Cycle, "I'm not making this up, you know." Robert's letter goes right in there with Lois's.

When the singers with whom I work complain that their upcoming engagement is the last one they'll ever have and that their career will be over next Tuesday, I always tell them to hang on, that Wednesday the phone will ring with a great new engagement offer. I had hardly hung up the phone from my dismissal from the CBC when I got a message from Dalhousie University in Halifax asking me if I would accept an honorary Doctorate of Laws, their highest honour. Naturally, I was thrilled and accepted immediately. (I'm sure my father, who was a lawyer, is up in heaven snorting, "Doctor of Laws? You barely made it through high school.")

In May of 2008, I went (accompanied by my sister Dorothy, who had briefly attended Dalhousie during the Second World War) to Halifax to receive my award. I was to give the commencement address, and I was very nervous. I had played for Maureen several times when she received some of her more than thirty honorary degrees, and I always found the ceremonies very moving and solemn. Several of my Toronto friends made the trip to Halifax to attend and to help me celebrate after the event.

I started my address by sharing with the audience my favourite quotation. A Scottish gentleman once said to the English composer Sir Arnold Bax, "You know, Sir Arnold, I think it's important to try everything in life at least once, everything, that is, except incest and folk-dancing." The audience roared with laughter and I stole a glance at the Chancellor. As he was laughing, as well, I relaxed, and was able to deliver the rest of my speech.

For the ceremony, I was dressed in a formal black suit, but the next day I gave a master class for the singers in the music department, and for this I reverted to my usual fetish fashions — leather uniform and riding boots. On the way back to my hotel, a young man approached me and said, "Hey, man, I saw your speech yesterday. You're really old, but you're cool." I choked out a few words and he went on. "But I'm sure glad we don't have to pay for your fashion statement."

Well, I seem to have bumped up against the present in my little dissertation. The problem with reading a biography is that when you begin, you know what's going to happen at the end. With an autobiography, or a memoir or reflections or whatever you want to call this book, things are somewhat looser. Mind you, by the time you reach your eighties, the tomb yawns, but I'm not there quite yet.

I've had a fabulous life. I've lived through a remarkable period in Canadian music. When I was a kid, music in Canada was totally dominated by English musicians, or musicians trained in England. After the Second World War, everything changed. Opera, which had been looked on as a decidedly second-class type of music, finally came into its own. From no opera companies in 1945 to the plethora of first-rate organizations we have now, Canada has taken its place in the world of opera with a vengeance. The opera world would be a much poorer place if all the Canadian-born and trained singers were to disappear.

It's been a great privilege to be a part of this transformation. I couldn't have asked for a more satisfying and rewarding career. I've always found the present to be better than the past, and even though my sex life was not so hot and my romantic life non-existent, I've been passionately in love with my singers — all ten thousand of them (perhaps that number is somewhat hypothetical).

I have a large group of dear and caring friends, I've had excellent health, and I've never had a major operation. I have lived with my sister Dorothy for over forty years and we've never had a fight. I've never had to hire a lawyer, and though I'm certainly not wealthy, unless the Canadian economy goes to hell in a handbag (although in 2008–09 it gave a very convincing appearance of doing just that), I should have enough to get me through to the grave. What's more, I have so far managed to stay on the right side of the tax man.

But best of all, I've been a musician. I've worked for Mozart, Verdi, Wagner, Debussy, and all those other kids — the best in the world. What more could one ask for?

During the last three years, in order to keep my brain from atrophying in my old age, I've memorized the play *Phèdre* by Racine, *en français*. Although

I can't honestly claim to be totally bilingual, my francophone friends pretend to enjoy it when I do it for them. Recently, I did the first two acts for an elderly lady friend of mine. When I came to the end of Act 2, she was fast asleep. I think that's what you call a riveting performance.

It has never been, and it's not now, an easy thing to be an artist in Canada. Unless one is among the very first class of performers — people like Glenn Gould, Jon Vickers, Maureen Forrester, or today Richard Margison, Ben Heppner, or Isabel Bayrakdarian — it is still a big struggle to make a living in this vast and underpopulated country.

But the talent is there. I go across this land every year, giving master classes to vocal departments of the various universities and young artists programs of the various opera companies, and everywhere there are eager little beavers pushing up in the music world. My friend Nancy Hermiston has, in an incredibly short period, made the vocal department of the University of British Columbia in Vancouver into one of the major centres for vocal study in the country. The opera department of the Faculty of the University of Toronto, the Glenn Gould Professional School at the Royal Conservatory in Toronto, and the voice department at McGill University in Montreal are all filled with kids who have the potential to become Canada's next cultural heroes.

I recently had a very moving experience. I was asked to give a master class for a group of semi-professional singers who were presenting Offenbach's *The Tales of Hoffmann* in an old church in Toronto's west end. I knew none of the singers, but they all turned out to be healthy, intelligent young artists eager to learn, and at least two of them had the possibility of developing major careers. After the class, they all thanked me, and several of them said that it had been like someone opening a window onto their roles. Thanks, Mr. Guerrero.

I'm a very good coach, I know that. However, no one teacher is right for everyone and I've had my failures. A good example of this took place a few years ago when a beautiful and brilliantly talented young woman came to me to coach the role of Lakmé in Delibes's opera. I pointed out to her that the first act of the opera is very interestingly constructed. We are introduced to the character of Lakmé first, in her public function as a priestess, a daughter of the Brahman High Priest. She leads a group of worshipers in a prayer. Next, we see her as a charming friend to her servant, Malika, when they sing the famous duet "Dôme Épais," and finally, in her aria, "Pourquoi dans les grandes bois," we see a young girl, trembling on the brink of womanhood. Then, when she is confronted with Gerald, an English soldier who has fallen in love with her, their duet recapitulates the three manifestations of her character that we have already seen. At first, as a sacred person, she rejects Gerald, then, as he passionately declares his love, she tries to warn him of the danger he is running in pursuing her, and finally, she confesses her love for him.

After our lesson was finished, this singer confessed to a friend (who hastened to tell me) that she couldn't understand what I was asking her to do. She apparently found the whole experience disturbing and she wasn't planning to have any more lessons with me. She is now having a lovely career in Europe where, presumably, she's not being asked to think about how *Lakmé* is put together.

That was one window that stayed firmly shut.

In March of 2002, I sat on a jury of elimination for a prestigious international vocal competition. The jury was totally "blind" — that is, we knew absolutely nothing about the singers whose tapes we were listening to. After we had reduced the 280 singers entered in the competition to twenty-one finalists, we were informed that fourteen of the singers chosen were Canadians.

All of this is stimulating and exciting and, as always, and I feel like the luckiest person in the world to be part of it.

In May of 2002, I played my last public concert. It went well (I've finally figured out how to do it), but sixty years of playing in public is enough. I've begun to have a bit of arthritis in my left hand, and Dr. Dupuytren has made an emphatic return visit to my right. However, the most important reason for stopping is that I find the concentration necessary to play a concert is now exhausting in a way that it never was before. I honestly don't miss performing, and I usually hire a pianist for my coaching lessons now. I love sitting back while everyone else is working hard, and I can play Buddha, the All-Knowing, and not worry about notes.

I always had something to say musically, although my execution of the music I loved was never exactly what I might have wanted. I've always said that I could do anything as long as it didn't have to be right. For that reason, I never used a script for my radio appearances. (Howard Dyck's ability to read scripts without a hitch is still mind-boggling for me.) By the same token, as a pianist I was never famous for my right notes. A good friend and valued colleague said to me recently, "Stuart, it's true that you never really could play worth a damn, but when you played, you had allure." I took that as a compliment.

I have no plans to retire. The great German soprano Irmgard Seefried once said, "You don't have a career in music, you have a life in music." As long as there is a soprano out there who wants to learn "Un bel dì" or the "Jewel Song," I'll be in there pushing and grunting till the end.

Shortly after writing that last sentence, I received a phone call from Lorna MacDonald, the Lois Marshall Chair of Voice at the University of Toronto. Part of her work as the Chair is to keep Lois's name and reputation alive for young singers. Appallingly, not fifteen years after her death, there are already kids who don't know who she was. Lorna is doing a great job and her call was to ask me if I would join her and mezzo-soprano Kimberly Barber in recreating the recital that I did with Lois and Maureen Forrester thirty-five years before at Massey Hall. At first, I refused. I haven't played in public now for seven years and my hands are not in such great shape. However, Lorna is a very persuasive lady, so I agreed to look at the repertoire to see if I could still manage it. As I began to practise, all the old enthusiasm came back and I had a thrilling time remembering the things that Guerrero had told me and which I never had had time to put to use. I agreed to do the two concerts that Lorna had arranged. After a couple of months of work (I can only manage about two hours of practising a day), I have the recital in my fingers again. This work has got me re-enthused about the piano and I'm planning to take some lessons with the magnificent Russian pianist Boris Zarankin who, along with his wife, Inna Perkis, has established a highly successful concert series here in Toronto. I'm working on a Mozart sonata and some of my old Debussy pieces.

Mozart and Debussy! It's like having a bath in Paradise. It will be interesting to see if Paradise is as good as working for these men. That is, assuming I get there.

(P.S.: The duet recital duly took place and was a grand success. There was a big house, and everyone seemed to have a great time. And, dear Emmy, I played the right notes!)

Afterword

I Spoke Too Soon

Since I finished writing this book a couple of years ago, I've had a heart attack, a triple bypass, open-heart surgery, and two other major surgeries. As I said to a friend recently, "When you get into your eighties, you wake up in the morning and you're grateful when nothing has fallen off, plugged up, or hemorrhaged," all of which have happened to me recently. However, these days I'm practising Bach on the piano, which makes up for a lot. (That old guy really knew what he was doing!) I'm also learning Fauré's exquisite F-sharp Major Ballade and two zippy Spanish pieces by Albeniz.

All I can do is paraphrase Schubert who, in his song "To Music," says, "In how many grey times you have sustained me. You Holy Art, I thank you from the bottom of my heart."

Index

Page numbers indicating images/captions are displayed in italics

Of Related Interest

True Tales from the Mad, Mad, Mad World of Opera
Lotfi Mansouri
9781459705159
$29.99

Everything about opera is larger than life, but the bigger the art form, the bigger the potential for disaster. When things go wrong at the opera house, they really go wrong. No one has a greater or more intimate knowledge of such moments than Lotfi Mansouri. This collection of discrete vignettes recount unforgettable and revealing moments at the opera as personally experienced or witnessed by the author. From unbelievable snafus to unfortunate mishaps to astounding coincidences, these vignettes feature some of the biggest names in opera. From the hilarious to the bizarre, this is a reader-friendly look at what is often thought of as an overly serious, even mysterious form of art.

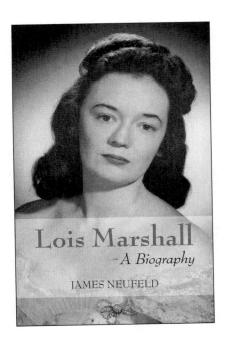

Lois Marshall
A *Biography*
James Neufeld
9781554884698
$28.99

Soprano Lois Marshall (1925–1997) became a household name across Canada during her 34-year career. This first-ever biography recounts her dazzling career and paints an intimate portrait of the woman, her childhood encounter with polio, and her complex relationship with her teacher and mentor, Weldon Kilburn.

Jan Rubes
A Man of Many Talents
Ezra Schabas
9781550026856
$40.00

Jan Rubes has been a leading performer and director on stage, film, and TV, and in concert, opera, musical comedy, and drama. With an operatic career already established, the Czechoslovakia native immigrated to Canada in 1949 and was soon the leading bass in the Canadian Opera Company. He helped develop the Young People's Theatre in Toronto. A member of the Order of Canada and holder of two honorary doctorates, he has won Geminis for his film work. His life is rich in detail — he has been both a national tennis champion and an important part of the history of the performing arts in Canada.